"When the rug is ripped from beneath everything you've known, you can spend the rest of your life trying to get over it. But a very different outcome is possible. In *Shaken: What's Next When Your Parents Are Splitting Up?* Debra Burns touches on a subject thousands of teens and young adults are struggling with—she does so with deep compassion, practical wisdom, and spiritual insight. I highly recommend this study for professionals, small groups, and hurting individuals. If you feel shaken, open these pages to find real hope and healing."

—ANITA AGERS-BROOKS, common trauma expert
and bestselling author of *Getting Through What You Can't Get Over*

"After 27 years of working with teenagers, Debra Burns realized this generation does not have a safe place to deal with challenges and the emotional pain it causes. She has created one of the first books to guide teenagers through heartbreak and leads them to hope for a better future. Anyone involved in the development of teenagers will appreciate the practical and insightful topics this resource provides."

—YVONNE S. KENNEDY, Ph.D., C.P
Vice President, Gateway Community Service

"Debra has provided an inclusive, evidence-based book that does an excellent job of incorporating the factual and the faith-based in an approachable format. The biggest message in all of this is that of hope—that you are not alone, and you can get through this with the help of others. I wish I had this when I was a teen going through my own struggles! This is a great resource for teens and for the leaders helping them walk through it."

—R. MICHAEL STAPLETON, Jr. M.A., LMHC,
Stapleton Consulting Services, Inc.

"This wounded generation does not have a safe place to take the emotional pain that comes in life. On the other side of their shame, anger, and confusion they will find healing and forgiveness. Debra's extensive ministry experience has prepared her for writing this invaluable workbook that we can all learn from. My greatest desire is that every young person carrying the burden and brokenness of life's challenges will find solace in this workbook and realize our loving God will not waste their pain."

—ANDREA KRAZEISE, Founder and Executive Director
The Pregnancy Center of Sanford/Oviedo/Winter Park, FL

"Since meeting Debra through her church partnership with Live the Life, she has been a huge advocate to support healthy families and marriages. She has led several workshops for Live the Life that have impacted not just the marriage but the whole family. Her desire to help the next generation build positive, strong relationships is the foundation for her work. This workbook is a wonderful tool for anyone working with youth, not only to help them process their feelings about their family dynamics, but to give them practical advice about their future relationships and marriage."

—MIEKO PAIGE, Live the Life,
Marriage and Family Program Manager

"We have enjoyed using past editions of Debra's course in our teen classes. The improved organization and depth of relevant content continues to challenge how we can help. As class leaders we are thankful that this tool can help us minister to those teens going through the pain and hurt caused by parental divorce."

—STEVE AND KIM BLAKE, Christian Family Chapel

"Many individuals of this generation are hurting and searching for peace, healing, and love. During a time of hurting, we have people such as Debra who get it and can offer a light in a dark time. This workbook is an opportunity to work through your pain and brokenness and come out on the other side knowing you are not alone."

—DR. MADISON NICHOLS,
Head of School Christ's Church Academy, Jacksonville, FL.

SHAKEN

WHAT'S NEXT WHEN YOUR PARENTS ARE SPLITTING UP?

A PRACTICAL AND BIBLICAL GUIDE FOR TEENS 13–19

DEBRA BURNS

With love,
Debra Burns

BROOKSTONE
PUBLISHING GROUP

ISBN: 978-1-949856-36-1 (paperback), 978-1-949856-40-8 (epub)

Printed in the United States of America

BROOKSTONE
PUBLISHING GROUP

Published by Brookstone Publishing Group

P.O. Box 211
Evington, VA 24550

Unless otherwise indicated, all Scripture quotations are taken from the Holy Bible, New Living Translation, copyright © 1996, 2004, 2015 by Tyndale House Foundation. Used by permission of Tyndale House Publishers, Carol Stream, Illinois 60188. All rights reserved.

Scripture quotations taken from The Holy Bible, New International Version® NIV® Copyright © 1973 1978 1984 2011 by Biblica, Inc. TM. Used by permission. All rights reserved worldwide.

Original research for material began in 2013 from a variety of sources. While we have taken every precaution to ensure that the content of this book is both current and accurate, errors and omissions can occur. Contact author for clarification. Debra Burns assumes no responsibility or liability for any errors or omissions in the content of this material.

Cover Design: Jonathan Lewis

Dedicated to
Autumn, Joshua, and Hannah.
You were my inspiration.
I wrote this for you and your generation.

CONTENTS

Stand firm &
be **Strong**
in your faith.
Remember that your family
of believers all over the **World**
Is going through
the same kind of
suffering
You are.

After you have
suffered a little while,
God will restore,
& **support,** & strengthen you
& He will place you on a
firm foundation.

My purpose in **Writing you is to** encourage you & assure you that what you are **Experiencing is truly** part of God's grace for you.

Stand firm in this grace &you will be unshakable

Based on 1 Peter 5:9–12

What Others Are Saying

66 I don't want to get married because I don't want to go through a divorce like my parents. IT'S JUST TOO PAINFUL." —*Monica, 13*

66 When I get married, DIVORCE IS NOT AN OPTION. I don't want to put my future kid in a situation I had to live in." —*Brett, 14*

66 It affects trust, that people won't do what they say they will. It affects my view of loyalty as well. EVERYONE CAN BE SO EASILY REPLACED." —*Autumn, 17*

66 I believe marriage does not last because PEOPLE GIVE UP ON EACH OTHER. I'm afraid people will not accept me if they know everything about me." —*Noelle, 16*

66 Divorce turned me AGAINST THE IDEA OF MARRIAGE. I didn't think marriages could really last forever. It took me years to come around." —*Shelli, 18*

66 I felt for a long time I didn't know what love meant. I tried to find love by dating a lot of girls, but the feelings never stayed very long. I'm afraid of marriage because I DON'T KNOW HOW TO KEEP FEELING LOVED." —*Derrick, 18*

How This Book Helped Others

66 I've learned that ANGER WILL EAT YOU ALIVE AND THAT FORGIVENESS WILL SET YOU FREE. You have to learn to accept people for what they have done." —*Matt, 13*

66 I've learned HOW TO DEAL WITH MY FEELINGS IN A GOOD WAY. I will be more conscious of how I act and what I say, as well as my outlook towards my parents' divorce. I've resolved some unfinished business with my feelings. I can sleep better at night. This has surpassed my expectations." —*Jake, 17*

66 I learned to GIVE ALL MY EMOTIONS TO GOD. This has helped me turn to God with every problem." —*Samantha, 13*

66 I learned that I CAN'T CHANGE WHAT HAPPENED IN THE PAST, but I can give my family a better life in the future." —*Derrick, 15*

66 DON'T ISOLATE YOURSELF, hang out with friends and people that love God. Know that many others deal with it too." —*Andrew, 17*

66 You can MAINTAIN A HEALTHY RELATIONSHIP WITH EACH OF YOUR PARENTS, even if they can't maintain one with each other." —*Jennifer, 15*

66 I've learned that MARRIAGE IS ONE OF THE BEST GIFTS GOD GIVES US, and to not let my parents' divorce affect my own views on marriage." —*Cora, 16*

From the Author

Through my years of working with students, I encountered many who feared marriage, because they didn't want to suffer a painful breakup. They asked questions like:

- *What is love?*
- *Why do people get married?*
- *How do I deal with this anger inside?*
- *Will my family ever feel normal again?*

- *How can I get along with new family members?*
- *How can I love someone unconditionally for the rest of my life?*

These are great questions but sound impossible to answer. I know, I thought so, too. If you can relate to the questions listed above and have more on your mind, I wrote this workbook to offer you hope. I want to answer your questions, prepare you for life, and to set you free from pain that no longer needs to be stuffed or ignored. I believe with all my heart, God can show you how to develop healthy, loving relationships. My goal is to help you know what I wish I knew growing up. If only I could protect you from pain, heartache, and disappointment.

After twenty years mentoring teenagers, I found it impossible to protect them from disappointment in life. But I believe through the support of a caring adult leading you through this material, the power of prayer, and the truth from God's Word, you will find comfort through this season of your life.

The heartaches and trials you endure are part of what makes you who you are and prepares you to face whatever may come. Painful experiences can be used to help others who need to hear your story. The transferable concepts you will learn and apply throughout this workbook will prepare you for life and equip you to help your friends, too.

I know you are not here by accident and appreciate that you are taking this wise and mature step to get help. It is my hope that you will build your life on a firm foundation. No matter what happens in your future, you will not be shaken.

Sincerely,

Debra Burns

Introduction

Our goal is to offer support, help you deal with your hurts, discover hope for the future, and experience God's love.

Dealing with your parents' divorce or separation can prove a very difficult time in your life. Divorce has affected the majority of this generation. Statistics show that in the U.S. alone, 50% of first marriages, 67% of second, and 74% of third marriages end in divorce. I noticed a lack of resources for teens to get the information, support, and guidance they needed during such a challenging time.

Whether your family breakup occurred a long time ago or recently, you may still need to process your feelings and emotions. Maybe you want to ask questions about what to expect, or you need to know how to adjust to a new stepfamily. Whatever your concerns—you are not alone.

Designed specifically to help you better understand your thoughts and feelings about your situation, this workbook will provide practical tips and guide you to a healthy view of life and relationships. This study will offer a brighter hope for your future. Whether you choose to use this book on your own or with a small group, I believe the material offers many benefits with your needs in mind.

You may find the experience of divorce easier to handle when you have someone to share it with. In group, the goal is to offer a safe environment where you can interact with one another, process the material, and build supportive friendships as you apply the biblical principles to your lives.

WHO THIS WORKBOOK IS FOR

Written to help middle and high school students ages 13–19, this workbook addresses questions, issues, and emotions teenagers may struggle with. Whether their parents never married, separated, divorced years ago, or are currently in the process of divorce, this book is designed to provide practical, emotional, and spiritual support.

Some aspects of divorce apply to everyone who faces it, but other issues vary from family to family. This workbook offers stories from teens who faced and worked through the disintegration of their own families. In some cases, divorce offers a positive solution to an abusive situation. But grief and pain abound when families break up for any reason. Each chapter of this workbook offers helpful information to speak to your family's unique needs, although some chapters may not apply to your specific situation. The differences among your small group bring opportunities to learn from the perspective of others with situations different than yours. By putting yourself in the shoes of another, you can better understand feelings and relate to people. Being able to hear, validate, and appreciate the experience of someone else will help create a safe discussion group where everyone can learn and grow.

HOW THIS WORKBOOK WORKS BEST

You may choose to use this workbook for your own personal study or with a family member. It also works well in small group settings of students led by a counselor, teacher, mentor, youth pastor, or other adults. Plan on 60–90 minutes for your group to meet. Whether administered in a coed or single-gender group, the study depends on the gathering's size and the students ages and comfort levels. Siblings may prefer to attend separate groups. Older students can impact younger students in a positive way by giving hope and examples of real-life experiences.

The study does not require homework. This workbook includes principles offered to students struggling with the impact of divorce. Introduce each chapter according to the needs of the students, not necessarily in the order given. Consider the unique needs of the students each week. Provided are suggestions to keep your group engaged and interactive with bonus material at the end of each chapter to enhance your study. After the first week, you may want to begin the meeting with each member sharing the high or low from their week to build rapport and trust within the group, then ask a review question from the previous chapter. At the end of each meeting, leave time for sharing and recording prayer requests and praises. The suggested prayer provided in each chapter can help students learn how to pray.

HOW TO USE THIS BOOK

Prayer Request and Praise Report

Leaders: Each week, encourage your group to share prayer requests and answered prayers to demonstrate the importance of depending on God. Ask them to write down each other's requests in the space provided and pray for one another throughout the week. Remind them of the confidentiality pact so they know not to share personal needs with anyone outside of the group.

Closing Prayer

We want to encourage you to begin praying at the end of each chapter. Whether doing this with a group or on your own, these prayers will help you put words to what you may want to say. They are only suggested prayers. Feel free to pray how you feel led. You can write out your own prayers to God below or in a journal.

GROUP GUIDELINES

....

Share: We all learn from each other's experiences and we encourage you to share yours. There is great healing that can happen when we build a community of trust and respect.

Maintain Confidentially: A simple rule to remember is, "What is said here, stays here." To help develop an atmosphere of trust, please do not talk about things you hear in the group to people outside the group.

Listen: When someone else is speaking, focus on what that person is saying in order to learn, comfort, and help. Remember not to talk when someone is sharing. Active listening means you are intentionally hearing what they are saying, not thinking about what you are going to say next.

Be Sensitive: Some of you may feel a bit shy and may not want to talk a lot. Try to participate, even if you tend to be quiet in groups. While some of you are naturally outgoing and comfortable sharing your feelings, make sure you don't dominate the group and talk too much. Some may feel uncomfortable with silence, but it's okay to give each other time to think about answers and contribute to the group, once you have had time to process your thoughts.

Be Open: Keep an open mind to the new ideas and information you will learn from this workbook. Also be open to everyone in the group who comes from different situations and backgrounds. We show respect by remaining openminded and listening with open hearts to find understanding and common ground.

Be Committed: Make a commitment to show up ready to learn and participate. This process is a journey, and you are part of the healing process for others, as well as for yourself. Your presence is important, and we need you to attend regularly. Every week is unique. We don't want you to miss out on what you can learn from the group, and what you contribute, in every session.

TIPS FOR LEADING SMALL GROUPS

First of all, thank you for investing your time to help teenagers during a difficult season. Facilitating a small group of teenagers has unique challenges because they are all at different phases of maturity. Some teens will not talk about feelings, while others will share too much and try to monopolize the meeting. When students are uncomfortable, they may joke around and distract the group from the topic at hand. It's important to redirect the conversation to stay on topic. The quiet ones are observing how you handle the group and how you respond to others sharing. They are weighing the pros and cons of opening up before trusting you and the group.

Don't panic if teenagers do not want to talk too much in the beginning. You may need extra time for them to warm up as you start every meeting. That is why we provided a few questions to review from the previous chapter before launching into a new topic. You never know how their day was or what kind of homework, stress, or family drama happened before they walked in to join your group on any given night. We have provided helpful and relevant bonus material at the end of each chapter to help fill your time in the 60–90 minutes allotted.

The task is to keep teenagers engaged and feeling safe enough to open up and share in a positive and friendly environment. They don't need to hear a list of dos and don'ts. They honestly don't want your advice until you've earned their respect. A popular saying you may have heard before bears repeating, "They don't care how much you know, until they know how much you care."

You can show your concern by maintaining curiosity ("tell me more") and by asking follow-up questions after they share a little bit. This keeps them talking.

Responding with empathy ("that must be tough") and not advice or a solution, will keep them engaged in open communication. By modeling empathy, you will show participants how to put themselves in the shoes of others so they can validate feelings and connect with people. You want to encourage each person to share joys, pains, heartaches, and experiences, without fear of rejection or ridicule. Their egos are very fragile, and sarcasm or harsh joking can crush a teenager's spirit. They may shut down and hesitate to open up again.

Focus on listening and demonstrating how to become an active listener to the rest of the group. When someone shares something heavy and serious, it's okay to have silence and let the weight of what they shared affect the students. Be patient when they are thinking about their answers. Teenagers need time to process their thoughts. Don't rush to the next question or ask too many questions in a row. Be okay with silence. Don't fill the air with chatter when they need time to think.

If you have a quiet teenager that does not want to participate, give them a few weeks to ease into it. Try asking them easy, general questions and save deeper questions for other students who like to share. The quiet ones are still learning and growing from observing discussions and following along in the workbook. Do not pressure them to speak but encourage participation when you sense they are ready.

If you have enough students, break up into a guy's group and a girl's group. This may help participants discuss the material with more emotional safety. Smaller groups also facilitate bonding and compassion for one another. This group will move toward a deeper understanding of each other as they learn to show respect and compassion for one another.

CHAPTER 1

What's Your Story?

"My mom had five husbands and lots of different men in her life between marriages. I grew up moving around so much that I went to five different middle schools in three years. My mom was more focused on her boyfriends and husbands instead of taking care of my sister and me. I missed out on a childhood because I had to take care of my sister. We both felt like excess baggage—dumped at strangers' houses. We slept on couches. There was no room for us. No thought about meeting our basic needs. I couldn't wait to grow up and get out on my own.

When I met my sister's friend one day, I knew she was the girl for me. I was 17 at the time and I knew I wanted to marry her. Her father told me no and said I would have to wait because she was younger. I waited 'til she graduated high school to ask her, but she wasn't ready to get married. I went off to the military but we kept in touch. One weekend on leave, I proposed to her and she said yes. We actually got married that very weekend and we've been together ever since.

I knew I wanted a different life than what my mom and dad had. I was determined to make a family for myself that I could be proud of and treat my future children with love."

The Lord is close to the brokenhearted & Rescues those whose Spirits are crushed.

Psalm 34:18

Leaders, please go over the group guidelines at the beginning of the first few meetings to set the expectations and boundaries. To help your small group get to know each other easily, start the first meeting with some general questions. Help students find common interests and build rapport, so the following weeks are built on a solid foundation. You can print the following questions on strips of paper and have each participant draw one at random to answer.

GETTING TO KNOW YOU

What is your favorite

movie? _____

food _____

restaurant_____

music_____

animal _____

snack _____

TV show _____

What do you do for fun?

_____

_____

_____

What is your favorite school subject and why?

_____

_____

_____

What is your least favorite subject and why?

_____

_____

_____

Introduction

What school activities are you involved in?

_____

_____

_____

Who is someone you admire and why?

_____

_____

_____

If you could go anywhere, where would you go and why?

_____

_____

_____

What do you want to do when you grow up?

_____

_____

_____

If you could meet anyone in the whole world, who would you like to meet?

_____

_____

_____

What is the most embarrassing thing that has ever happened to you?

_____

_____

_____

LET'S GET STARTED

· ·

Going through the experience of your parents' split up or divorce is a challenging time of change that comes with a variety of emotions. While it may be one of the hardest things you ever do, it is possible to make it more manageable by practicing two important things:

1. Find people to help you.

2. Express your thoughts and feelings with them.

What have you been thinking and feeling since you found out about coming to this group?

_____

_____

_____

Write the two things that will help you through this time.

_____

_____

_____

Sharing your experience will help you heal and understand why you feel the way you do. Some teenagers have described feeling numb, shock, embarrassed, consumed with thinking about parental separation, angry, devastated, ripped apart, a loss of hope, grief, disconnectedness, and can't focus or concentrate on schoolwork. Can you relate to any of these? Are you feeling a wide range of emotions and have no energy to get out of bed?

Why do you think divorce hurts so much?

Divorce is one of the most painful things you can go through—almost as bad as death of a loved one. Emotions are unpredictable, but they are manageable.

Sometimes, it's hard to find the right words to say when sharing your story. I've provided a guide to help you articulate your feelings so you can choose more descriptive words other than mad, sad, or happy. Frustrated, disappointed, and confused, are also words you can add to your vocabulary to clearly express yourself to others.

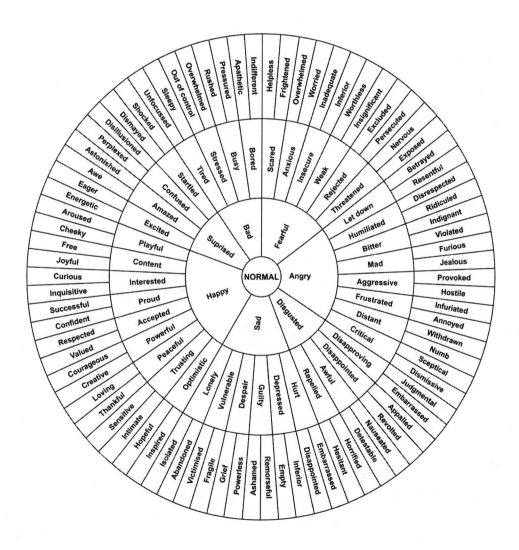

If you are using this workbook in a small group setting with people you don't know yet, these questions will help you get to know each other.

- Who is in your family?

- Who do you live with currently?

- What do you think about your parents' decision to divorce?

- If your parents had asked for your opinion before they made their decision, what would you have told them?

- Who have you been able to talk to about this so far? i.e. teacher, friend, family member, coach.

There are sections of the Bible that can help us learn how to deal with our emotions, worries, and questions.

It is often said the BIBLE could stand for:

Basic
Instructions
Before
Leaving
Earth

Another way we like to think of the Bible is

The owners manual for life.

Read Psalm 31:9–10 (NLT):

Have mercy on me, Lord *for I am in distress,* tears blur my eyes. **My body and soul are** *withering away. I am dying* from grief. My years are shortened by *Sadness. Sin has drained* *my strength* **I am wasting away** from within. Psalm 31:9-10

What emotions from this scripture can you relate to, because of your family's situation?

_____

_____

_____

How are David's emotions affecting him physically? Have you noticed any physical affects from your emotions?

_____

_____

_____

God wants us to come to Him with our problems. He is always available to you and He can handle your emotions. You don't have to stuff your feelings. He wants you to share your pain, disappointments, and anything that concerns you.

PRAYER REQUEST & PRAISE REPORTS

Write down prayer requests in the space provided and pray for one another during the week.

I know the Lord
is always with me.
I will not be
Shaken
for he is
Right beside me.

Psalm 16:8

CLOSING PRAYER

Dear God,

Help me understand what is going on in my life right now. I need you to guide me through this difficult time. Please give me wisdom to know what to do and the courage to do it. Please lead me to the right people to help me. Teach me to trust you and trust others who want to help me. Thank you for giving me enough faith for today. Please help my faith grow through this. God, I pray you work all this out for good. Help me to be open to this process. In Jesus' name. Amen.

The Lord
is close to the
Brokenhearted
&
Rescues
those whose spirits are
Crushed.
Psalm 34:18

Next week we will look at how your unique family situations may have you feeling overwhelmed and what you can do about it.

Is the Divorce My Fault?

Have you ever felt responsible for your parents' breakup or divorce?

_____

_____

_____

66 I THOUGHT IT WAS MY FAULT because of the way my parents treated me when they were angry at each other." –*Derrick, 19*

66 I keep thinking about WHAT I MIGHT HAVE DONE that caused my parents to argue, or ways I could have helped (like cleaning the house), that would have prevented an argument. I believe those arguments are the reason they are splitting." –*Noelle, 21*

66 I thought I was the center of the world, especially my parents' world. So, when my parents split IT MUST HAVE BEEN MY FAULT." –*Autumn, 20*

66 They never told me THE REAL REASON THEY BROKE UP, so I drew the conclusion that I was involved, somehow. My parents still won't tell me anything about it." –*Jake, 19*

66 I think some kids have to have something to blame and so they choose themselves, WHICH ISN'T FAIR AT ALL TO THEM." –*Kai, 16*

Would you feel comfortable talking to your parents about how you feel?

_____

_____

_____

15

CHAPTER 2

What Do I Do
When I Feel Overwhelmed?

MELISSA'S STORY

"I miss the family we used to be. When I was twelve, my dad started drinking too much. He would come home angry and violent almost every day which led to a lot of yelling and fighting. It wasn't always like this.

"I had a good childhood and many happy memories. My dad used to be funny and annoyingly happy. After a year of fighting, my mom had enough, and we packed up and left him. It was hard on us financially. I could tell my mom was stressed, angry, and depressed. We stayed with friends and in hotels for a long time. I hated living out of a suitcase and wearing the same clothes all the time. I hoped my friends at school wouldn't notice or say anything. I didn't want anyone to know. I wasn't motivated to work hard at school and lost interest in hanging out with friends. Moving around so much made it hard for me to keep track of stuff and I would lose things, like schoolwork, often. We never had money for anything fun. I guess you can say I was grieving for all I had lost. I wish I never knew the family life I was missing out on, because this change just made it worse."

My purpose is to give them a Rich & Satisfying life.
John 10:10

Leaders: Begin your small group by asking each member to share a high and low from the previous week. Try to limit stories to one minute or less. You can even use a timer to help students learn to articulate their stories in a brief and concise manner. Share about your life briefly too, in order for the students to get to know you. Lead into a personal example of feeling overwhelmed to begin this week's lesson.

ARE YOU FEELING OVERWHELMED?

According to Melissa's story what do you think made her feel confused and overwhelmed?

Make a list of any thoughts and feelings that are confusing you because of your parents' divorce.

_____

_____

_____

Medical experts tell us when we are emotionally overwhelmed, our inner health is affected. We lose energy and interest in meeting the basic needs in our daily lives. Our emotions and state of mind become completely overshadowed by weariness.

How can you tell when you are emotionally overwhelmed?

_____

_____

_____

How should we respond when we recognize this in our own lives?

_____

_____

_____

We are on this path with you, working together to help with your emotions. Here are ten reasons why you may feel overwhelmed, and suggestions for what you can do about it.

USE THESE WORDS TO FILL IN THE BLANKS.	
Hear	Numb
Sleep	Under
Sick	Focus
Fun	Alone
Feel	Moody

1. YOU CAN'T _____

You become confused at school, forget where you put things, or completely space out during an important activity. Trying to learn a new video game or focus on reading a book seems taxing, almost impossible. You may lose the capacity for routine tasks such as brushing your teeth or remembering to add shampoo to your hair.

> **What you can do about it:** During overwhelming brain freeze, it's important to realize you're probably not losing your mind. You are just overwhelmed by the stresses of life and the burdens of others. Take a deep breath. Make a list and slowly accomplish one thing at a time. Give yourself grace and ask forgiveness when you forget your best friend's name.

What ways are you losing focus?

_____

_____

_____

What action steps can you take to help you concentrate better?

_____

_____

_____

2. **YOU CAN'T** _____

Although you may feel exhausted by the burdens you bear, restful sleep seems as far away as next year's summer vacation. You wake up in the middle of the night, worry about the latest problem or fight at home and try to pass the time looking at social media on your phone. You climb out of bed and pace for a while until you feel tired enough to try sleep again.

> **What you can do about it:** Keep the electronics away from your nightstand and turn off the computer at least one hour before bedtime. Before you climb into bed, cast every care on the One who never sleeps. Ask God to deal with any problems while you rest. Breathe deeply and focus on the peace Christ promised us. Try not to let troubles climb into bed with you (John 14:1). *"Don't let your hearts be troubled. Trust in God, and trust also in me."*

How many hours of sleep are you getting at night? _____

Do you feel rested when you wake up? _____

What changes to your sleeping habits can you make this week?

_____

_____

_____

3. I _____ IMPATIENT

Waiting in line at the store or waiting for a commercial to finish starts driving you nuts. You are easily frustrated, and your temper is out of control. You are desperate for help with your math homework, but your parents don't understand basic algebra. Your coach adds another practice to an already overloaded calendar. Impatience makes us snap, because peace has left the building.

> **What you can do about it:** Give yourself extra time to get things done. Don't overpromise anything or overextend yourself. Fight against perfectionism which can lead to self-doubt and self-sabotage. It's important to learn to protect your emotional energy and to wisely choose how you spend your time. Staying up until 3:00 a.m. listening to a friend, will leave you physically and emotionally drained.

How are you a perfectionist about some things in your life?

_____

_____

_____

How can you begin to protect your emotional energy?

_____

_____

_____

What changes do you want to make this week?

_____

_____

_____

4. I CAN'T _____ FROM GOD

Praying to God is the last thing on your mind. You don't feel like your prayers are reaching the ceiling over your bed anyway, so what's the point, right? We've all been there. It may feel like the One who promised to never leave us seems to have checked out. Not wanting to talk to God or listen to Him is a frustrating place to be.

What you can do about it: When you are overwhelmed and just can't seem to pray, remember David from the Bible. There were times in the Bible when we are told David was in distress and wondered if he did something wrong that kept God away from him. David was an example of a man who was very close to God. David is known for being, *"a man after God's own heart."* But even David had bad days and struggled with praying to God.

Look at how David prayed in his despair from Psalm 143:1,4–6, *"Hear my prayer, O LORD; listen to my plea! Answer me because you are faithful and righteous. I am losing all hope; I am paralyzed with fear. I remember the days of old. I ponder all your great works and think about what you have done. I lift my hands to you in prayer. I thirst for you as parched land thirsts for rain."*

Notice how David was losing hope and was paralyzed with fear. He was honest with God and waited on God to respond. Just as David was loved by God, know that you are precious to God too. This season you may be going through is not your fault. When you're emotionally exhausted, it's difficult to communicate with anyone: friends, siblings, parents, even your Yorkie Terrier. When you can't pray, it's a signal from your soul—time to schedule a retreat and get away from all the mess and get into the presence of God. Play worship music and get some private time to clear your head of negative thoughts, so you can focus on God. Read from Psalms each day and see how you can relate to the anguish David felt at times.

What do you think is hindering your desire to pray?

_____

_____

_____

Who could you ask for help, or to hold you accountable to begin praying regularly?

_____

_____

_____

5. I AM _____ TOO MUCH PRESSURE

Maybe the pressure from your soccer team, your grades, and your social life are all piling on too many demands. We know the struggle can feel like a heavy blanket. With your parents splitting, the future is unknown, finances have changed, and living arrangements are changing, too. So many people with too many problems. Shoulders feel tight and a migraine threatens. The pressure to keep it together is overwhelming.

> **What you can do about it:** Talk to a close friend, someone you can trust. Release the burdens and let your friend help you pray. When Moses felt the burdens of battle, Aaron and Hur supported him by lifting his hands (Exodus 17). They were beside him for the duration. Their strength added to his power and they won the battle together. Learn from Aaron and Hur's example in Exodus and try not to do it all on your own. Ask for help.

How many things are you committed to currently? _____

Are you overcommitted to too many things? _____

If you could remove one thing out of your life that is causing pressure, what would it be?

_____

_____

_____

6. I WANT TO BE LEFT _____

When your emotional tank is empty, it's hard to be around happy, bubbly people who love life. Isolating yourself in your room sounds like an easy way to escape the noise of others who feel like emotional rollercoasters. Sometimes you just want to get off by yourself and escape their ups and downs. It's okay to retreat in moderation, just be careful not to hide out for days at a time.

> **What you can do about it:** It's time to build healthy boundaries. The word "no" is just as spiritual as, "Sure, I'll help." You don't have to answer every text or read through every email. Take a nap, read a book, listen to music. Learn how to care for yourself and avoid feeling pressure to fake it, so you can make others happy.

How much time do you spend alone?

_____

_____

_____

Do you think this is healthy for you or would you like help finding things to do with others?

_____

_____

_____

7. **I BECOME** _____

A snarky attitude begins to take over. You even find yourself snapping at your innocent dog for following you around. The negative emotions you bottle up are trying to spill out. They need a release valve. If you don't do something soon, you will either explode or you'll stuff, it which can lead to more painful consequences.

> **What you can do about it:** It's time to do something physical. Go to the gym and beat on a punching bag or punch a pillow in your room. Take a brisk walk around the block—alone or with a friend. Talk out your emotions as you walk. You could even beat a cardboard box around the back yard using a baseball bat and label the box with the name of a situation (or person) causing you pain. Participating in exercise or a team sport will help relieve stress. The physical activity will help take your mind off what is stressing you and release a natural chemical called endorphins that make you feel better and may help change your mood.

How can you take control of your moods?

_____

_____

_____

What physical activity can you add to your schedule this week to lift your mood?

_____

_____

_____

8. **I FEEL** _____

The numbness caused by being emotionally overwhelmed is actually more dangerous than moodiness or the expression of negative behaviors. Numbing means you've internalized the emotions and now you're in danger of major problems. You find yourself trying to self-medicate and doing things you never would have imagined. You suddenly realize you are in trouble.

> **What you can do about it:** Find a credible counselor, someone you can trust and someone who is skilled. This may help you get over the hump and give you the ability to function.

❝ You cannot selectively numb. If we numb anxiety and uncertainty, we also numb joy, love and creativity. You are imperfect and wired for struggle, but you are worthy of love and belonging." There is another way to allow ourselves to be seen. Deeply seen. To love with our whole hearts even with no guarantee."

—BRENE BROWN

WAYS WE NUMB

- *Focusing on others' needs*
- *Staying busy / Acquiring things*
- *Minimizing / Self-invalidating*

- *Screens and Substances*
- *Overcontrol / Perfectionism*
- *Anger / Lashing Out*

List the top 3 ways you tend to numb out:

_____

_____

_____

What are 3 other things you can do instead of numbing out:

_____

_____

_____

9. **I STOPPED HAVING _____**

Your friends want to go to a movie or out for pizza, but you just want to take a nap. The family wants to schedule a vacation, but you can't think of a single place you want to go. Game night becomes boring. The usual TV show that makes you laugh now offers no relief. You can't remember the last time you laughed out loud.

> **What you can do about it:** Make just one change. Sometimes one change begins a steppingstone of transition to help you release some of the stress. Even a change in routine might bring back some enjoyment in life: a different coffee shop, a new outfit, a fun hair color. That single action may help you make it through a difficult season.

Even if your family seems to be falling apart, you have permission to take a break from all the drama and have fun. What do you think is holding you back from letting yourself enjoy life?

_____

_____

_____

What steps can you take this week to add some fun into your life?

_____

_____

_____

10. **I GET _____ A LOT**

A series of colds or flu or a strange virus suddenly attacks. This can happen even months after the emotional trauma from the family divorce or breakup. The body has carried too much for too long and becomes toxic. The body unloads those emotional poisons. Unfortunately, many of us wait too long for this wake-up call.

> **What you can do about it:** Pay attention now to the rest your body needs. Take care of yourself with regular doctor visits and proper nutrition. Eating nuts, fruits and vegetables is healing, even a magnesium supplement can help restore energy. Make daily exercise a priority. Self-care is a vital physical, emotional, and spiritual discipline. Physical exercise may help release the tension you feel when there is stress. Participating in some form of exercise will help you cope with the stressful feelings you experience.

When was the last time you went to the doctor for a checkup?

_____

_____

_____

Have you been feeling sick and physically overwhelmed with all that is going on in your life?

_____

_____

_____

When will you talk to your parents about how you are feeling and make a plan to see a doctor?

_____

_____

_____

Throughout life you may face different levels of emotional stress. You can learn to be proactive with your time and with your choices. You can protect your heart from becoming emotionally overwhelmed and can live more abundantly with joy. God wants you to have a full and abundant life.

PRAYER REQUEST & PRAISE REPORTS

Write down prayer requests in the space provided and pray for one another during the week.

CLOSING PRAYER

Dear God,

There are big changes happening in my family. I am worried about a lot of things and need your help. I feel like I have to carry the burden alone. Words like overwhelmed, confused, stressed, and tired seem to describe what I'm feeling. I am not sure how to let you carry my heavy load, so please show me how. Take it from me. I pray you give me patience when I need it and help me communicate my needs and feelings with my family. Thank you, God, that I will never be alone even when I feel lonely. In Jesus' name. Amen.

Besides feeling overwhelmed, you may also feel a deep sadness. Next week we will look at the symtoms of grief and learn how to process the pain of grief.

Replacing Tension and Stress

If there is enough time, you can use this activity to help students evaluate activities they may enjoy when they feel emotionally overwhelmed.

The list below describes a number of physical activities that may help release tension and stress caused by family situations. Put a star by the activities you currently enjoy. Put a check mark next to any activities you would like to try. Place an "x" by the ones that you are not interested in doing at this time.

☐ archery	☐ baseball	☐ basketball	☐ cricket
☐ diving	☐ dance	☐ bowling	☐ gymnastics
☐ hiking	☐ hockey	☐ golf	☐ karate
☐ tennis	☐ biking	☐ skiing	☐ swimming
☐ wrestling	☐ paintball	☐ laser tag	☐ water-skiing
☐ lacrosse	☐ soccer	☐ football	☐ surfing
☐ paddle boarding	☐ skin boarding	☐ kickboxing	☐ weightlifting

Write down other physical activities you enjoy.

_____

_____

_____

Regular exercise can help prevent stress levels from rising out of control. From your list above, which activities would you like to do on a regular basis for preventing stress?

_____

_____

_____

What Do I Do When I Feel Overwhelmed?

Tell us when and where you could fit these activities into your routine.

_____

_____

_____

List any activities you could do when stress rises unexpectedly.

_____

_____

_____

Try not to set your goals too high, so you have trouble meeting them. Be sure to set exercise goals that are realistic and manageable for your skill level and time availability.

TEN TIPS FOR WHEN YOU START FEELING OVERWHELMED

· ·

1. When it's hard to focus and concentrate on schoolwork and details, you may be emotionally overwhelmed. Pay attention and be aware of the warning signs.

2. When you can't sleep, keep the electronics away from your nightstand and turn off the computer at least one hour before bedtime. Before you climb into bed, cast every care on God.

3. When you feel impatient and get frustrated easily, don't overcommit to things and stress yourself out. Manage your time wisely.

4. When you feel like you can't pray to God, schedule a retreat to get alone with God and focus on reading the Bible and worshipping Him.

5. When you feel overburdened, talk to a friend you can trust. Pray with someone.

6. When you don't want to be around people, give yourself permission to take a break for a few hours to gather your thoughts, journal, or pray. A short amount of time alone is a natural way to cope with overwhelming emotions, just don't withdraw too much or for too long.

7. Are you cranky? That means it's time to get physical. Go for a walk or burn some calories at the gym or in the pool. Blow off some steam.

8. Not feeling anything at all? This too can be a warning sign that you are emotionally overwhelmed. It's time to get some help and talk to a trusted counselor to help you process your emotions.

9. Are you not enjoying life to the fullest? God wants you to have joy even in the midst of a tough situation. Give yourself permission to go have fun. Get a new pet, a new haircut, or find a new activity or sport to try.

10. Are you feeling sick? Take care of yourself with regular doctor visits, physical activity, and proper nutrition.

CHAPTER 3

How Do I Deal with Loss?

ASHLEY'S STORY

"Some friends and family members made me feel like my pain doesn't matter. Even though my parents divorced a long time ago, they did not understand my loss and wanted it to remain ancient history. They would tell me to 'get over it' or to 'get on with my life.'

"I've had to learn to ignore any messages like this. I gave myself permission to grieve.

"My counselor said to me, 'Your loss has shaken your life, and it takes some time to pick up the pieces and find a way to put them back together again. Don't hurry yourself or let anyone rush you.'

"I suggest you share the pain of your grief with safe people who will listen to you and appreciate what you have gone through with your broken family. Each time you open up and share, you're letting go of a little more hurt and allowing a little more healing to take place. That's the way grief goes—a little at a time, day by day, for as long as it takes. So, give yourself permission to open up to healing one step at a time."

For my thoughts are not your thoughts, Neither are your ways my ways.
Isaiah 55:8

Leaders: Open with a question every group member can answer. For instance: "Have you ever lost something important to you? How long did you look for it? Where did you find it? If you didn't find it, is it irreplaceable?"

Share an example from your life where you lost something important to you or a dream that you had as a young person that did not pan out the way you wanted it to.

THE LOSS OF A DREAM

Divorce is in many ways like a death. When a family is broken it can have a deep impact on each family member. The loss of a dream and unmet expectations can cause great disappointment. It can feel devastating and unfair.

When things change in our lives, something is always lost. Even if you still see both of your parents and know they each love you, the way your family once existed is different. It is normal to feel grief when you experience loss.

UNDERSTANDING AND GRIEVING MY LOSS

Mourning the breakup of your family because of divorce or separation may be a new concept you never thought of before. The emotions that grief causes after any loss are completely normal. When things change in our lives, something is always missing. Any loss can trigger mourning. In this chapter we will discuss the stages of grief by Elizabeth Kubler-Ross, M. D., author of the internationally best-selling book, *On Death and Dying* (1969). In this timeless classic, she shares her theory of the five stages of grief, also known as the *Kübler-Ross model.*

Denial, anger, bargaining, depression, and acceptance make up the five stages of grief, as outlined by Kubler-Ross. For our purposes, we have added blame and forgiveness as they relate to dealing with divorce. It's important to know you may not experience one step, complete it, and then move on to the next. You may pass through the various stages in any order and repeat one or more of them again and again. One friend described it like this: "The stages of grief are like having a bouncy ball in a box hitting every side in a random manner. You never know what stage is coming next."

STAGES OF GRIEF

· ·

USE THESE WORDS TO FILL IN THE BLANKS.
Anger Denial Bargaining

STAGE 1: _____

This stage doesn't tend to last long, but most people go through it. You may think things such as, "This can't be happening to me," or "This can't be real." Sometimes people ignore the situation altogether by spending more time with others, watching TV, playing video games, reading novels, etc. Anything to escape reality is a form of denial. Choosing to ignore reality is not a healthy way to cope.

What other ways of coping have you tried, aside from denial?

_____

_____

_____

What do you think is the next stage people go through when grieving a family breakup?

_____

_____

_____

STAGE 2: _____

You feel upset that your parents are getting a divorce. During this stage you may push others away from you or you may be difficult to be around. You might experience thoughts like, *how could they do this to me?* You are mad at them or their marriage counselor or other people who you believe may have caused or not prevented the separation. You may even feel angry at God or the world for allowing this to happen.

What other reason would someone have to feel angry about the situation they are going through?

_____

_____

_____

On a scale from one to ten, how angry do you feel about your parents' separation or divorce?

_____

_____

_____

What is the third stage grieving people go through when the family unit changes?

_____

_____

_____

STAGE 3: _____

This is where you begin to accept that the divorce is going to happen, but you want to put it off a little longer. You may think, *I'll be a great kid if they don't divorce*, or *Just let them wait until I finish high school.* Maybe you try to talk your parents out of the divorce. Wanting to maintain control of the situation will lead to pain, exhaustion, and ultimately disappointment.

In what ways have you tried to bargain with your parents to get them to change their minds?

_____

_____

_____

How have you tried to regain or maintain control of the situation?

_____

_____

_____

We will discuss the next few stages in the Kubler-Ross model of grief in our next section.

Oh God, your ways are holy
Is there any god as Mighty as you?
You are the God of Great
Wonders
You demonstrate your
Awesome Power.

Psalm 77:13-14

PRAYER REQUEST & PRAISE REPORTS

Write down prayer requests in the space provided and pray for one another during the week.

I know the Lord
is always with me.
I will not be
Shaken
for he is
Right beside me.

Psalm 16:8

CLOSING PRAYER

Dear God,

Divorce feels like someone or something died. This is unfair. I am hurting and confused. I have a lot to process and I need you to help me. Please give me strength and comfort when I feel isolated in this. I know I'm not alone because you are with me and the Bible says you give me peace. What do I have to fear? You are in control. Please God, help me let go of trying to control everything. Help me let go of fear and receive your peace. In Jesus' name. Amen.

with a *Gift*—
PEACE of **Mind**
So & **Heart**
don't be
Troubled
or **Afraid** John 14:27

Facing the different stages of grief brings healing and makes you stronger! This next lessen in grief gives you power to face whatever comes your way. Keep diving in!

CHAPTER 4

Why Does This Feel Like Grief?

"Silence doesn't bring freedom. I would suggest finding a safe person to talk with about things happening at home or within your own mind and heart. Find someone who can compassionately listen, and who will help you in your healing process.

Also, allow yourself time to grieve. You have to go into the pain of the loss to get through it. Even the negative emotions are crucial in the healing stages (anger, sadness, etc.), because they signal your mind that you are losing something you value, something you believed in. Denying and suppressing those feelings is like ignoring the things that mean something to you, in this case your parents, others who are affected, and your concept of marriage."

Consider it all **JOY** when **YOU ENCOUNTER VARIOUS TRIALS,** knowing that the testing of your **FAITH** produces Perseverance. Let **PERSEVERANCE FINISH ITS WORK** so that you may be mature, **PERFECT** & Complete, Not lacking anything.
James 1:2-4

Leaders: *After the students share their highs and lows, begin this week with a follow up question from the previous week. Have you thought any more about the stages of grief? Did you experience any new feelings this week that you were not aware of before we discussed grieving? If so, what have you noticed? How did you deal with new emotions?*

TIMELINE FOR YOUR GRIEF

Most people require two to three years to do all their necessary grieving. Some may take more, and some may take less, because there's no one-size-fits-all timeframe for mourning. You are unique, and your personal timeline for grief is the only one that matters for your situation.

How long you mourn depends on a variety of different circumstances in your life. How much support you've received from people around you, how many changes have taken place because of the divorce, and probably a thousand other variables.

Now, we'll continue sharing the stages of grief from the previous chapter. We already covered denial, anger, and bargaining, so let's discuss the other four common symptoms of family loss.

USE THESE WORDS TO FILL IN THE BLANKS.
Blame
Acceptance
Forgiveness
Depression

STAGE 4: _____

At this point you realize that not only are your parents going to divorce, but you can't prevent or delay it. You may feel sad and cry a lot, or not feel like doing some of the things you used to enjoy. During this stage, you may think, *Nothing will ever be the same again—why bother with anything?* or *What's the point of life?* Unfortunately, that's pretty normal.

This is an important stage of grieving. Depression is not something others should try to cheer you out of. You're dealing with the divorce in your own way and in your own timing. You can't rush through the stages. It's okay to let yourself feel these feelings. However, if you get stuck in this stage, which we will discuss further in this study, or any of the previous stages, you may need to see a counselor or a psychologist for help and support.

Have you noticed any feelings of depression during this season in your life?

_____

_____

_____

On a scale from one to ten, how depressed are you feeling today?

_____

_____

_____

In the past, what has helped you overcome feelings of depression?

_____

_____

_____

STAGE 5: _____

As a teenager, the stuff you're dealing with may be so overwhelming, all you can possibly wrap your head around is that someone must be responsible! Thoughts at this stage often come as automatic reactions. *My mom was too busy with church. My dad was away working too much. My parent is a cheater! It's my fault because my mom/dad was so involved in my school or sports activities.*

> Remember: You are NOT responsible for your parents' decisions. However, blame often serves as a "quick fix" that leaves you feeling more in control. This is especially tempting when you feel you have no say in the decisions your parents are making.

Do you feel like you don't have a voice about what is going on in your family? How does that make you feel?

_____

_____

_____

Have you had thoughts of blaming someone for what is happening?

_____

_____

_____

But the Lord's plans
stand firm forever,
His intentions
can never be
SHAKEN
Psalm 33:11

STAGE 6: _____

In the acceptance stage, you understand that the divorce is going to happen, and you know you'll have to adjust to it. This doesn't necessarily mean you'll be happy with the outcome, and you may still want to be left alone for a while. You may think, *If I can't fight it, I might as well prepare for it*, or *Everything will be okay in the end*. Once you accept your parents' decision to live separately, you may start feeling like you are getting out of the pit of despair. Emotions are lifting and you are able to accept the new normal that now makes up your family dynamic.

Acceptance means coming to terms with the arrangement of your parents' split. How has this stage of grief affected you?

_____

_____

_____

What do you tell yourself when you are facing the facts and accepting their decision?

_____

_____

_____

The Lord is close to the Brokenhearted & Rescues those whose spirits are Crushed.
Psalm 34:18

STAGE 7: _____

This is where you decide to forgive your parents and anyone else you felt held responsibility for the divorce. Forgiveness is a choice not a feeling. You may never feel like forgiving the one who disrupted your life and caused all of this change. Let's face it, one or more of your parents may not deserve grace. They may even continue hurting you over and over again! Forgiveness can even seem pointless if your parent doesn't seem to care. Choosing to release anger, frustration, or resentment helps the forgiver heal, even if the other person does not ask for forgiveness. It is a vital step in your healing process. More on forgiveness will be covered in following chapters.

Are there any people in your life who have hurt you—people you are struggling to forgive?

_____

_____

_____

If so, what is blocking you from releasing your emotions?

_____

_____

_____

BE KIND TO EACH OTHER, *TENDERHEARTED* FORGIVING ONE ANOTHER *Just as God through* CHRIST HAS FORGIVEN YOU

EPH. 4:32

DISCUSSION QUESTIONS

••

- Which stage or stages of grief have you experienced so far?

  _____

  _____

  _____

- Which stage of grief do you think you are in now?

  _____

  _____

  _____

- Make a list identifying your personal losses as a result of your parents' separation or divorce.

  _____

  _____

  _____

- How did you handle the divorce or separation, or how are you handling it now?

  _____

  _____

  _____

- What expectations did you have when your parents told you they were getting divorced? How did reality differ from those expectations?

  _____

  _____

  _____

HEALTHY PROCESSING

∙∙∙

Allow yourself to come through grief in your own way. There is no time limit. Healthy mourning requires a dose of reality. You can't run from your need to process your pain or escape it. Don't numb yourself and self-medicate by implementing unhealthy coping skills that only add to your problems and won't work anyway.

In death there is closure after the memorial or funeral service. Your grief is significant and comes in waves, but you can process the pain in a manner that eventually heals over time. With divorce, when you are bounced between shared custody, you may continually leave a parent every weekend or every other week for years. That leaving creates a constant reminder of loss and causes fresh emotional wounds over and over again. You are still involved with your parents, but you are no longer a whole unit in the way it was before.

FACING YOUR THOUGHTS AND FEELINGS CAN HELP YOU HEAL FASTER

∙∙∙

Sometimes you have to feel bad before you can feel better. I am referring to Autumn's advice in the beginning of the chapter, where she said, "*Allow yourself time to grieve, you have to go into the pain of the loss to get through it. Negative emotions are crucial in the healing stages because they are a signal to your mind that you are losing something you value. Denying and suppressing those feelings is like ignoring the things that mean something to you.*"

Journaling is an action to get your thoughts and emotions out of your head and on paper. Do you have a journal?

Or will finding another avenue for expressing yourself work better for you? Pets are great for bringing comfort, joy, love, and support. You never have to worry about a pet telling someone else your private thoughts without permission. You can talk to them anytime about anything.

Do you have a pet? Would you consider getting a pet if you don't have one? What kind of pet would you like?

It probably doesn't feel like it, but there is value in this season of your life. Not one tear is lost. Even better than a pet, God is there for you—anytime and anywhere—to listen, care, and comfort you. God will take every bit of your pain and mold it in His hands. He will bring good out of this unwanted circumstance.

PRAYER REQUEST & PRAISE REPORTS

Write down prayer requests in the space provided and pray for one another during the week.

Stand firm
in this grace
& you will be
unshakable

Based on 1 Peter 5:9-12

CLOSING PRAYER

Dear God,

I need your peace to guard my heart and mind right now. I have a lot of different feelings throughout the day and I just feel emotionally drained. Please comfort me and give me strength to face what is happening in my family. I can't go through this alone. Please use this challenge in my life to make me who you created me to be. Even if you can't change my circumstance, then change me. In Jesus' name. Amen.

Then you will experience God's PEACE WHICH EXCEEDS anything we can understand. His peace will guard your hearts & your minds as you live in Christ Jesus.
Phil 4:7

8 Coping Skills to Deal with Pain

Everyone experiences mourning differently. It is normal for grief to come and go—one day you might think it's all gone, and the next day you feel bad again. The following ideas have helped people cope with their pain. Check any that you think might help you.

☐ **EXPRESS YOUR FEELINGS.** Talk or write about your grief in a way that feels safe to you.

☐ **TAKE YOUR MIND OFF YOUR PAIN.** Listen to music, go to a movie, play a sport, or spend time with friends.

☐ **DEVELOP A SUPPORT NETWORK.** Make a list of people you feel comfortable going to when you feel like you need company.

☐ **COUNT YOUR BLESSINGS** and write down what you have gained because of your parents' divorce. Think about what you still have: your health, education, talents and skills, hobbies, friends, and faith.

☐ **FOCUS ON WHAT YOU CAN CONTROL** instead of what is out of your control. You can still choose who your friends are, how you spend your free time, what activities you want to participate in, and what you want to do with your future.

☐ **TAKE CARE OF YOURSELF.** Self-care is important when you feel overwhelmed with grief. It can be physically and emotionally draining. Getting enough sleep and exercise and eating well can help keep you feeling strong and healthy.

☐ **AVOID SELF-MEDICATING WITH ADDICTIVE SUBSTANCES** like alcohol, drugs, and food. They may provide a temporary escape from your feelings, but addictions will not allow you to heal and will bring much greater consequences in the long run.

☐ **ALLOW YOURSELF TIME TO RECOVER AND ADJUST.** Be patient with yourself. Divorce creates a big change in your life.

CHAPTER 5

Will I Ever Trust Again?

TOMMY'S STORY

"I was so mad at the world, at my parents, and even at God for my family breaking up. It's not supposed to be like this. I never thought it would happen to my family. My parents were involved at church and took my sister and I to everything they offered.

When Mom and Dad told me about taking time to separate and we stopped going to church as a family, I lost all interest in going, too. I was embarrassed and did not want my friends from youth group to know what was going on at my house. I didn't trust people to keep from spreading rumors. I tried not to think about it or talk about it with the hope my parents would change their minds and work things out. The divorce was not final for a long time, so being in limbo gave me hope that maybe something would change. I tried to pray, but God didn't seem to hear my prayers, let alone answer them. I gave up on trusting God and turned my back on faith and church."

For you created my innermost being; you knit me together in my mother's womb. I praise you because I am **fearfully & wonderfully** made; your works are **wonderful** I know that full well.
Psalm 139:13-14

49

Leaders: You may want to begin with reviewing prayer and praises from the previous week to follow up on participant concerns. Depending on the dynamics of your group and where they are emotionally and spiritually, you can choose to discuss this chapter this week or wait until group members are more open to the idea of discussing spiritual things. Try to find out where they are spiritually in a non-threatening way. Have an open mind to accept wherever they are on their spiritual journey. Opening the door to communicate about faith during week 4 will give you a foundation to build on during the next few weeks, if the group seems ready. You can begin by asking this question.

On a scale from one to ten, how sure are you God wants to help you?

66 Right beside my pain is my faith; it does not cancel my pain, but it does inform it. My faith calms my pain, provides perspective to it, and faith reminds it that this life is not all there is."

—RON L. DEAL, AUTHOR OF *THE SMART STEPFAMILY*

GOD DOES WANT TO HELP YOU

God wants to help you through this difficult time. You may not know much about God or even believe in God and that's okay. You may have a measure of faith, but still struggle with trusting in the goodness of God. That's realistic, too.

When your world feels upside down and your foundation is shaken, it can impact your faith. Some people may feel closer to God, while others feel He has abandoned them. It's okay to be honest with God. Tell Him how you really feel about your doubts, fears, and anger.

Some people find strength through their faith, while others reexamine or rethink their entire belief system during hard times, at least for a season. It's understandable. Trust has been broken. People have let you down. Your expectation of a forever family is gone and you are hurting.

You can lean on family and friends, but you also need a relationship with God, because He is your Creator. God is mindful of what you are going through. He thinks about you!

Read Psalm 8:3–4.

God can teach you how to love again. Love your family. Love yourself. Love others. And love God.

When I look at the *night sky* & see the work of your fingers the moon & the stars YOU SET IN PLACE – what are mere mortals that you should think about them human beings THAT YOU SHOULD care for them?
Psalm 8:3-4

> ### Where have you sought to get help during this complicated and difficult time in your life?

You could have chosen other options, but we are glad you are holding this workbook today. Have you thought about how God could help you through this?

On scale from one to ten how much do you trust God? _____

Wherever you are on your spiritual journey, you are not alone. You are never alone. God is with you. The principles we share in this study come from the Word of God. The Bible. We believe it is the one true source that brings hope and healing to every situation. Before you dive into this workbook, we believe it's important to consider a relationship with God through faith in Jesus Christ, so that the information in this study will make a real difference in your life.

Are you open to the idea that God (the Creator of the Universe) knows what you are going through, and that He could help you through this? Yes or no?

Read Psalm 139.

O Lord, you have examined my heart and know everything about me. You know when I sit down or stand up. You know my thoughts even when I'm far away. You know everything I do. You know what I am going to say even before I say it, Lord. You go before me and follow me. You place your hand of blessing on my head. Such knowledge is too wonderful for me, too great for me to understand! I can never escape from your Spirit! I can never get away from your presence!

On a scale from one to ten, how confident are you that God is aware of what you are thinking and feeling? _____

I would like to share four principles to help you know God's love. The information in this chapter may answer some questions you have.

THE FAMILY TREE

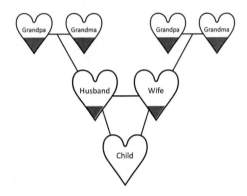

Let's imagine two people meet and fall in love. Each one came from two parents who may not have been the most loving and kind people in the world. Maybe their parents were unable to give and receive unconditional love. Their parents each created a baby, but their hearts were only half full. The two children that were made grew up in a broken and dysfunctional family. When these two grow up, they meet, fall in love, and create life (a baby) with a heart only a quarter full. The mom and dad have not learned how to give or receive love, so the cycle continues from one generation to the next.

What would your family tree look like? Take a minute to discuss or draw your own hearts and fill in how you think it would look at this time of your life.

> **Where do you think the child of the parents in the story receive the love they need to survive?**

What if I told you that God loves you and He has a wonderful plan for your life?

Read John 3:16.

For God so Loved
the WORLD
that He gave His
one and only SON
that whoever believes
in Him shall not **Perish**
BUT have eternal *Life*
John 3:16

Have you ever heard this before?

_____

_____

_____

What is the promise God makes to those who believe in His Son, Jesus Christ?

_____

_____

_____

What do you think prevents us from knowing God?

_____

_____

_____

ANOTHER FAMILY TREE

In the beginning Adam and Eve created life out of their love.

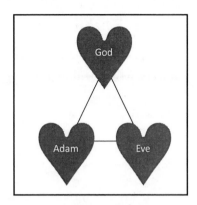

But when they sinned (disobeyed God) and brought death and brokenness into the world, they caused a huge separation between God and mankind. This story is in Genesis, the first book of the Bible. The first couple God created broke their relationship with God and brought sin into the world.

Later, in the New Testament part of the Bible, we learn that Jesus is the Son of God who died on the cross to overcome death, forgive us for all of our sin, and bring us into a right relationship with God so that mankind is no longer separated from God. Jesus takes away the sin in the world.

- You and I are part of the world and we are sinners, too. What do you think sin is?
- How does sin impact families today?

People are sinful and separated from God. Look at what Romans 3:23 NIV says.

For all have **sinned** & fall short of the *Glory of God.* Rom. 3:23

- According to this verse, how many people have sinned?

God is not surprised that you (and your parents) are not perfect and will make mistakes. For some people it's hard for them to admit that they need help from God. They only want to depend on themselves to meet all their needs. Usually independence is a good thing. Your parents want you to be an independent and mature adult one day. God wants that for you too, but He also wants

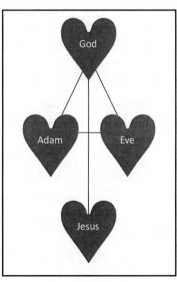

you to depend on Him. He is the source of true joy, peace, comfort, strength, and love. Especially love!

- What is the best gift you have ever received?
- What if I told you that God has a gift for you and it's totally free?

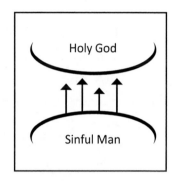

Forgiveness for all your sin is a major gift that God offers you.

Read Ephesians 2:8–9.

This verse and the diagram show that "sinful man" tries to reach God in their own efforts, but they can't reach a Holy God on their own.

- What are some ways people try to please God?
- How do you think we can reach a Holy God if we are sinful?

We need to acknowledge our sinfulness and take responsibility for our selfish ways. How do we do that? God's loving kindness leads us to "repentance." The word (repent) means there is a change of direction, you choose to take a new course. In life sometimes, there is a need to change direction and make a U-turn.

Look at what scripture says.

If you declare with your mouth, "Jesus is Lord," and believe in your heart that God raised him from the dead, you will be saved. For it is with your heart that you believe and are justified, and it is with your mouth that you profess your faith and are saved.

—Romans 10:9–10

God wants us to ask for forgiveness and believe in Jesus' sacrifice, then He receives us as His children into His family. In this diagram you see Jesus and the cross connecting God to His people. The arrow is showing

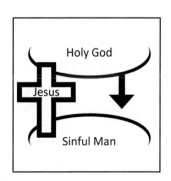

us that God initiates the relationship with mankind out of His great love for us.

Look at what John 1:12 NIV says.

No matter what your family looks like today, no matter how broken, God is inviting you into His family where He will be your Heavenly Father. Did you know all sin is equal in God's eyes? There is nothing God won't forgive.

We may think sin is measured like a typical chart or graph, but from God's perspective when He looks down at His children, all sin is like a level playing field.

The top of the graph looks the same.

When I asked God to show me the truth, I read John 14:6 in the Bible. "*Jesus answered, 'I am the way and the truth and the life. No one comes to the Father except through me.'*"

According to John 14:6, is there any other way to get to our Heavenly Father?

You may be wondering, *How do you invite Jesus to come into my life?*

Here is a simple prayer I prayed when I believed and wanted to be forgiven of my sin and surrender my life to God. There are no magic words. It's not about what you say as much as it is about your heart. God knows a sincere heart.

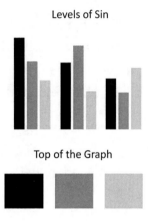

He gave the right to become Children of God.
John 1:12

Levels of Sin

Top of the Graph

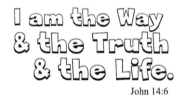

I am the Way & the Truth & the Life.
John 14:6

Dear God,

I need YOU. I'm sorry for my sins. I believe Jesus is the Son of God and died in my place because of my sin. I now invite Jesus to come into my life as my Savior and Lord. Thank you for forgiving me for all of my sins. Thank you for giving me eternal life in Heaven with you. Help me to accomplish every good work you have for me to do and help me become who you created me to be. In Jesus' name. Amen.

If you asked Christ into your life, you have made the most important decision you will ever make. Welcome to the family of God! Now what?

This is what the Bible says happens when we become a Christian or "Christ Follower."

I have been crucified with **CHRIST** & I no longer live, but **CHRIST** lives in me. The life I now live in the body, I live by **FAITH** in the Son of God, who **LOVED** me & **GAVE** Himself for me.
Gal. 2:20

Oh God, your ways are holy Is there any god as **Mighty** as you? You are the God of **Great Wonders** You demonstrate your **Awesome Power.**
Psalm 77:13-14

These two verses remind me of the transformation that happens when a caterpillar turns into a butterfly. A caterpillar and a butterfly look nothing alike after the transformation. I don't think a butterfly flies around missing being a caterpillar because he has a new life. He is a new creation. When Christ's Spirit is in us, we too become new creations. We may not change on the outside, but the change happens on the inside. The more we yield or surrender to the Holy Spirit the more transformation will happen in our lives.

WHO IS THE HOLY SPIRIT?

God the Father, Jesus Christ the Son, and the Holy Spirit make up the Trinity. Trinity means three in one. The way it was explained to me is how water, ice and steam are all made up of the chemical H2O. It comes in three forms just like God, Jesus, and the Holy Spirit.

The Holy Spirit is not a thing, it's the Spirit of Jesus Christ come to live inside every believer who accepts a relationship with Him. It's not a ghost or anything to be scared of. He comes in the form of a spirit to help us become more like Christ and fulfill our purpose on earth.

Look at what Jesus said to the disciples after He rose from the grave.

When you become a Christian, you may want to read the Bible and allow the Holy Spirit to help you understand what you are reading.

"But the Advocate, the Holy Spirit, whom the Father will send in my name, will teach you all things and will remind you of everything I have said to you" (John 14:26 NIV).

You will notice other changes too! I felt a sense of gratitude like no other when I asked Jesus to forgive me of my sins and accept me into God's family. I am just so thankful that He loves me and saved me from eternity apart from Him. Other changes happened, too.

1. You will have power to choose right over wrong.

2. He will guide and direct you to help you make the right decision.

3. He will let you know when you need to ask forgiveness for hurting someone's feelings or when you need to forgive someone else for hurting yours.

4. He will give you the power to obey God even when you don't feel like it.

The more you surrender to the Holy Spirit working in you, the more you will feel God's pleasure and delight over you. You bring God joy! Did you know that? When you are fully committed, devoted, and surrendered to God, He blesses you with His peace and love like nothing you have ever felt before.

If you are ready to make the commitment to Christ, let an adult know of your decision and talk to your parents first. If you are not ready to take that step of faith, that's okay too. Just know your group leader is available to discuss spiritual issues whenever you have questions.

DID YOU KNOW THAT YOUR FAMILY NEEDS YOU?

It's very normal to feel like you don't fit in sometimes. God knows you perfectly, yes, everything about you, and He loves you. God also knows your family. He put you in your family for a reason. God doesn't mean for bad stuff to happen to you. He hurts when families are broken, and people are hurting each other. He knows what you are going through, and He is with you through it all.

Psalm 139 in the Bible is a special poem written about how God created you.

O LORD, you have examined my heart and know everything about me. You know when I sit down or stand up. You know my thoughts even when I'm far away. You know everything I do. You know what I am going to say even before I say it, LORD. You go before me and follow me. You place your hand of blessing on my head. Such knowledge is too wonderful for me, too great for me to understand! I can never escape from your Spirit! I can never get away from your presence!

God is inviting you to be a part of His family by accepting His Son, Jesus Christ. You can pray a prayer to God to express your faith. Here is a prayer I prayed:

Dear Jesus,

I need you. Thank you for dying on the cross for my sins. I believe in you and I want to receive you as my Savior and Lord. Thank you for forgiving me of my sins and giving me the gift of the Holy Spirit to help me understand more about who you are. Take control of my life and make me the kind of person you created me to be. Thank you for letting me in God's family and giving me eternal life. In Jesus' name. Amen.

Does this prayer express the desire of your heart? If it does, pray this prayer now, and Christ will come into your life as He promised.

Through a relationship with God through Jesus, you will find comfort, help, guidance, love, encouragement, forgiveness and understanding. The list goes on and on. You have a role to play in God's family. Enjoy fulfilling your purpose, not just in your earthly family, but in the world, too!

PRAYER REQUEST & PRAISE REPORTS

Write down prayer requests in the space provided and pray for one another during the week.

I know the Lord is always with me. I will not be **Shaken** for he is Right beside me.

Psalm 16:8

CLOSING PRAYER

Dear God,

Help me to rest in the truth of Psalm 86:13, "Great is your love toward me." You already see the ways I will fall short and mess up. But right now, I receive your unconditional love for me. I recognize Your love for me is not based on my performance. You love me in spite of my weaknesses and sin. That's amazing. But what's most amazing is that the Savior of the world would desire a relationship with me. Lord, I want to believe. If there is any unbelief in me, take it away. In Jesus' name. Amen.

For you created my innermost being; you knit me together in my mother's womb. I praise you because I am *fearfully & wonderfully* made; your works are **wonderful** I know that full well.

Psalm 139:13-14

GET THIS 2.0

6 Tips to Rebuild Trust in Your Family

When your parents let you down and you feel it's hard to trust adults, the rebuilding of confidence takes time, patience, and work. It is a two-way street. They need to be able to trust you just as much as you need to trust them again. Demonstrating mutual respect can build trust if you are motivated. Here are some steps to help you learn to trust people again based on an article by Dr. Andrea Bonior Ph.D. in Psychology Today Dec. 2018, *Say What You Mean and Mean What You Say*.

You probably pick up very quickly when someone is saying things that aren't really true. When we are around people who lie, we adjust our behavior and expectations accordingly. When people don't follow through with what they say they are going to do, you learn not to trust the person quite as much the next time, in order to not be let down. So, if you are looking to increase trust with your parents and family members, it's imperative that you stop saying things you won't follow through on, or that don't represent your actual feelings. Being honest with yourself and others will help build trust. Even what seem like minor lies, will hinder the ability to trust one another.

1. BE VULNERABLE—GRADUALLY.

In most relationships it is important to build trust through vulnerability. Some of this comes automatically with time and daily interactions. Building trust takes a willingness to open yourself up to the potential risk of hurt. It's important to share parts of yourself with others gradually, once they have earned your trust. For instance, talking about something embarrassing from your past, letting people in on what scares you, admitting to areas about yourself you think are weaknesses, are all steps to see how the other person responds and protects your vulnerability. Trust is built when people have the opportunity to let you down or hurt you but do not. And in order for them to pass the test and build that confidence, you must make yourself vulnerable to that letdown. Gradually is best, of course, to protect yourself along the way.

2. REMEMBER THE ROLE OF RESPECT.

One of the most emotionally lasting ways relationships can hurt our trust is when we feel disrespected. Your opinions regarding family decisions matter and when you feel left out of the discussion, you may feel disrespected. Or you may lash out at your mother or father in ways that you never would with a stranger. Respect is even more important with your loved ones, because the lack of it can create damage over time. This does not mean you must be formal or perfectly polite with your family members every moment. But it does mean you must remember that every time you don't treat them respectfully, you harm your connection a bit, and it becomes more difficult for them to trust you.

3. GIVE THE BENEFIT OF THE DOUBT.

What goes hand in hand with trust is setting aside your doubts and letting the person come through for you. In relationships where trust has been broken, and you are trying to rebuild, it may not be wise to set aside all doubt all at once. But over time, if you hope to truly rebuild trust, you must be willing to string together some moments of letting the doubt go and see if the person comes through for you. (If they don't, then it is them who is sabotaging the trust-building.)

4. EXPRESS YOUR FEELINGS EVEN WHEN IT'S TOUGH.

Emotional intimacy comes in part from knowing that you can express your feelings to someone, and they will still care about you and will not dismiss you. They will show a willingness to listen. It means you know they will make time to understand your view-point, not to shut it down. This requires the maturity of being able to talk about feelings without escalating into shouting, verbally attacking, or getting defensive. Work on talking about difficult emotions that feel helpful and respectful. Learn to discuss challenging emotions in ways that don't automatically jump to feeling threatened or start a conflict. Handling conflict correctly can bring people closer together instead of driving them apart. Don't be afraid of tough conversations when feelings are involved. We will discuss more about conflict in another chapter.

5. TAKE A RISK TOGETHER.

Building trust can involve doing something new together as a family. Maybe an adventurous experience on a vacation, introducing healthier eating habits, learning a new sport, or discovering new hobbies together. This puts all of you outside your comfort zone with the possibility of reward in the form of increased trust.

6. BE WILLING TO GIVE AS WELL AS RECEIVE.

When there is a healthy level of trust in a relationship, you know you won't end up giving, giving, giving without the other person/people coming through for you in return. A significant component of building confidence is to let this process happen. Literally everyone understands that they're not supposed to always take more than they give. There is a balance necessary to establish trust and boundaries. Being willing to both give and receive, you create a comfortable, caring homelife where everyone feels valued and appreciated

CHAPTER 6

How Do I Deal with My Emotions?

SYDNEY'S STORY

"The reality of my family breaking up first hit me a few weeks after my dad left the house. I was at the store and it dawned on me. We were alone. Dad wasn't coming back. Everyone else was going on as if life was normal. All I could think was, *How can you act like nothing happened? My dad is gone, and I don't know what is going to happen. Life can never be normal again!* I ran to the bathroom crying. I didn't want to talk to anyone about it, hoping it would all go away and he would change his mind.

"I started getting headaches every day at school. When I put my head down on the desk, my teacher asked if I needed to go to the nurse. At the nurse's office she asked me what was going on at home, because she thought the headaches might be coming from all the tension I was holding inside. I broke down crying and finally told her about my parents' divorce. It felt good to let someone know how I cried at random times throughout the day and before bed. The nurse said it was normal to feel emotional. She understood there had been a major change in my life and said I wasn't used to it yet. She said it would take time and to find safe people to talk to. She asked if I had ever spoken with a counselor before. I said, 'No way. I would never do that. Kids would make fun of me.'

"The nurse said that seeing a counselor for help is not a sign of weakness, but of strength. It takes courage to face one's problems instead of hiding from them. She gave me the name of a counselor who had experience working with teens. My mom made an appointment for me the next week. Once I started talking with a counselor, I realized I was able to express my feelings and found healthy ways to deal with them. The counselor was a good listener and didn't judge me for my thoughts and feelings."

God knows how much
I LOVE YOU
& long for you with
the tender compassion of
CHRIST JESUS
Phil. 1:8

Leaders: Open with highs and lows from each group member. Ask a fun question to help start the meeting on a high note.

- *Share a funny story about something that happened at school recently.*
- *Share a time when you felt embarrassed or something happened that made everyone laugh out loud.*

Give the students time to think and reflect during the discussion time. This may be new and uncomfortable for some to open up about their feelings. Make sure it's a safe place for them to be authentic and honest. Remind the group of the confidentiality pact. Share an experience from your life that relates to emotions and how you felt.

DEALING WITH EMOTIONS

Maybe you've had a similar experience like Sydney's story. People around you are living as if everything is normal, but everything in not normal for you. Your world feels like it's turned upside down. Your emotional wounds may seem unbearable.

The pain you feel right now will not always be as intense and will not last forever. Let the reality of your loss sink in, as painful as that reality may be. You can only heal what you allow yourself to feel. Experiencing the feelings your loss has stirred up is one step toward healing.

You may go through different levels of sadness or depression when your parents divorce or separate. Depression is a deeper, more intense type of sadness. Some people get emotional when triggered by a TV commercial or song on the radio. They may lose focus while at school or lose interest in hanging out with friends. Others may have trouble getting out of bed in the morning, miss their bus, lose their appetite, skip school, and just lose energy to do the most basic things like brush their teeth.

You can help yourself manage these feelings by being aware of them, expressing them, taking action to find relief, and getting professional help if needed.

How Do I Deal with My Emotions?

Rate yourself on a scale from 1 to 10 below, according to how much you are experiencing these symptoms of sadness.

_ CRYING	_ GETTING INTO TROUBLE
_ NOT EATING WELL	_ FEELING HELPLESS
_ NOT SLEEPING	_ LOSING INTEREST IN ACTIVITIES
_ FEELING DOWN	
_ FEELING TIRED	_ LOSING FOCUS
_ NOT WANTING TO BE WITH FRIENDS	_ FEELING WORTHLESS
	_ FEELING GUILTY
_ STRESSED ABOUT THE FUTURE	_ FEELING FEARFUL OF THE UNKNOWN
_ LOSING INTEREST IN ACTIVITIES	_ LOSING INTEREST IN BEING AROUND FRIENDS
_ DROPPING GRADES	

DEPRESSION—WHAT IS IT?

Depression is an extreme sense of sadness triggered by your loss. Unfortunately, it is necessary for your healing. Depression is a natural response to loss.

USE THESE WORDS TO FILL IN THE BLANKS.	
Feels	Sadness
Hopelessness	Loss
Cares	Focus
View	Home
Sleep	Energy

1. Un-connectedness: feeling like nobody _____. Feeling ugly and unloved.

2. Profound sense of _____: crying, persistent sadness.

3. Hopelessness, pessimist: negative _____ of past, present and/or future.

4. Losing interest in favorite activities: wanting to stay _____ and mope.

5. Sleep routine disturbed: wanting to _____all the time or not being able to sleep.

6. Change in eating habits: binging or _____ of appetite.

7. Substantial loss of energy: daily activities take tremendous _____.

8. Hard to concentrate: the inability to _____ (grades start to slip).

9. Thoughts of suicide: sign of desperation and _____.

10. Impacts spiritual life: rethink spiritual beliefs, _____ abandoned by God.

Even people in the Bible struggled with depression.

Don't feel guilty. Depression is a healing emotion. Depression is not a sin. Depression is a natural reaction and is not sin.

Read how David felt when he wrote a prayer to God in Psalm 143:7–11:

Come quickly, Lord, and answer me, for my depression deepens. Don't turn away from me, or I will die. Let me hear of your unfailing love each morning, for I am trusting you. Show me where to walk, for I give myself to you. Rescue me from my enemies, Lord; I run to you to hide me. Teach me to do your will, for you are my God. May your gracious Spirit lead me forward on a firm footing. For the glory of your name, O Lord, preserve my life. Because of your faithfulness, bring me out of this distress.

GOD'S MEDICINE

· ·

Scripture is God's medicine and the recommended dose is 3 times a day with no harmful side effects. Seriously, applying the Word of God renews your mind and your thoughts will follow.

We are hard pressed on every side, but not crushed; perplexed, but not in despair; persecuted, but not abandoned; struck down, but not destroyed. —2 CORINTHIANS 4:8–9	*Praise be to the Father of compassion and the God of all comfort, who comforts us in all our troubles, so that we can comfort those in any trouble.* —2 CORINTHIANS 1:3–4
O Lord, I have come to you for protection; Be my rock of protection, a fortress where I will be safe. I entrust my spirit into your hand. Rescue me, Lord, for you are a faithful God. —PSALM 31:1–5	*The Lord says, "I will rescue those who love me. I will protect those who trust in my name. When they call on me, I will answer; I will be with them in trouble. I will rescue and honor them. I will reward them with a long life and give them my salvation."* —PSALM 91:14–16

How Do I Deal with My Emotions?

Describe what the writers of these Bible verses have in common.

_____

_____

_____

_____

What do these verses say about God?

_____

_____

_____

_____

How does God comfort those who are emotionally hurting?

_____

_____

_____

_____

How will you apply these verses to your circumstances?

_____

_____

_____

_____

EMOTIONAL HEALTH

Did you know 85% of energy is consumed by emotions. The goal to emotional health is finding balance in all areas: physical, mental, spiritual, and emotional. We are off balance when our emotions are consuming our energy.

WHY DOES IT TAKE SO LONG TO HEAL?

Friends may say, "Come on, get over it, get on with your life. It's no big deal."

When we have a weakened energy supply, it alters our ability to manage emotions. No one likes to hurt. So, we go to things to escape feeling hurt and pain. Some choose alcohol or drugs over exercise, too much time watching TV, or playing video games. All of these can be choices to numb out the pain. We need coping skills when we hurt. The coping skills you learn now as a teenager, will help you throughout your whole life when challenges arise.

Your parents may be giving into temptations to cope in unhealthy ways, too. You may see them make choices they would not have made if they were still married. This may rock your world to see your parents behaving in a way that is nothing like who they were before. For instance, they may be jumping into new relationships very quickly. Walking wounded into another relationship without healing from the divorce will cause more damage to them and possibly you. It will lead to more pain and a greater sense of loss.

EMOTIONAL STABILITY, WHERE DO WE FIND IT?

• •

Your faith and relationship with God will help significantly during this season of your life. Friendships help alleviate feeling lonely. Healthy friendships will lift your spirits and build you up. Finding a healthy support system is important, too.

Where do you find good quality friendships?

_____

_____

_____

Do you have a friend who will listen and pray with you and for you?

_____

_____

_____

Have you ever been a friend for someone else to offer support during their crisis?

_____

_____

_____

Do you know someone who may be hurting too, that you can walk through this together with?

_____

_____

_____

An active spiritual life will make a significant impact in your life. What does an active spiritual life look life for you personally?

_____

_____

_____

Do you need help to grow in your faith?

_____

_____

_____

How do you think faith helps you overcome the emotional stress you are experiencing?

_____

_____

_____

God is the only one who understands how deep the hurt feels. Be honest with God and let Him know how you are doing.

CHANGE YOUR FOCUS

Does it seem like the whole world is splitting apart? That would be frightening and unsettling for anyone. You may feel shaken like never before. You are not alone!

When you focus on changes that will take place when your parents get divorced, your thoughts produce feelings of despair and panic. When you switch your focus to things that will not change, your thoughts can produce feelings of greater peace and stability.

Write down as many things as you can come up with that are <u>not</u> changing because of the divorce.

_____

_____

_____

(Refer to this list whenever you start feeling unstable and anxious. Changing your focus will help bring you greater peace.)

Did you know there are 362 verses in the Bible about peace? The Bible is a great resource to help renew your mind and focus God's Word, too. Check out these three verses Paul writes to the Philippians in the New Testament on peace.

May God Our Father and the Lord JESUS CHRIST give you *Grace* & PEACE&
Phil.1:2

Then you will experience God's PEACE which exceeds anything we can understand His PEACE will guard your hearts and minds as you live in Christ Jesus.
Phil. 4:7

Keep putting into practice All you learned & received from me - everything you heard from me & saw me doing. Then the *God of* PEACE will be with you.
Phil. 4:9

What do these verses say about God?

_____

_____

How does God comfort those who are emotionally hurting?

_____

_____

How will you apply these verses to your circumstances?

_____

_____

WHAT OTHERS HAVE TO SAY:

66 I never thought growing up without my dad would have affected me so much like it did, but I know he loves me, and I've learned to deal with how our current relationship stands. I love my mom and dad and things are what they are. I don't hold it against either one of them. There are some issues that you will have to learn to get over and I know abandonment was a big one for me. But talking through the emotions and everything going on daily with a person I trusted, helped me get through it." *–Autumn*

66 It's okay to have all the feelings. Sad, angry, confused. Find a way to get them out, either through talking with a trusted adult, listening to music, writing about it, or something physical like sports or dance."*–Shelli*

Leaders: Students may be feeling complex emotions but not have the vocabulary to name what they're feeling beyond an elementary vocabulary like happy, sad, mad. Teaching the vocabulary to name emotions will be the first step to discover how to manage them. As the leader, be careful to not make assumptions about what a student does or does not feel based on gender, background, culture of family or how they have been taught to express those emotions. Many factors can lead a teenager to mask or hide feelings rather than process them. Give each student the space to talk openly and discover how emotions may affect them.

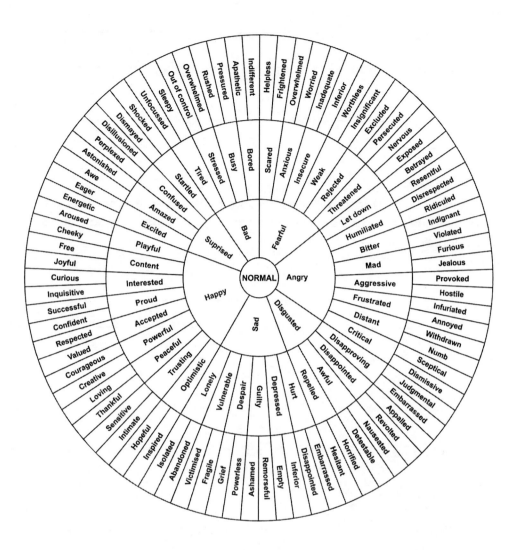

The Bible says Jesus was human and experienced the kinds of feelings and temptations you do. Because of Jesus, emotions don't have to control you. Emotions can be overwhelming; Jesus can help us keep them in check.

Using the Feelings Wheel provided, which of these emotions (in the center of the wheel) did you feel this week?

_____

_____

_____

_____

Which ones (in the outer circles) best describe the emotion you felt?

_____

_____

_____

_____

What is something that most people believe about emotions and how they should be expressed by girls, guys, older people, younger people?

_____

_____

_____

_____

The Bible says Jesus was human and experienced the kinds of feelings and temptations you do.

Read Matthew 26:36–39.

> *Then Jesus went with them to the olive grove called Gethsemane, and he said, "Sit here while I go over there to pray." He took Peter and Zebedee's two sons, James and John, and he became anguished and distressed. He told them, "My soul is crushed with grief to the point of death. Stay here and keep watch with me." He went on a little farther and bowed with his face to the ground, praying, "My Father! If it is possible, let this cup of suffering be taken away from me. Yet I want your will to be done, not mine."*

How Do I Deal with My Emotions?

Jesus knew He would soon be crucified so He went to a place where He could pray.

Describe how you think Jesus was feeling.

_____

_____

_____

What did Jesus do in response to those feelings?

_____

_____

_____

DON'T BE AFRAID,
for I am with you.
Don't be **DISCOURAGED,**
for I am your God.
I will strengthen you &
help you. I will hold you up
with my **victorious**
right hand.
Isa. 41:10

What is God's response when you reach out to Him?

_____

_____

_____

What was the greatest blessing you have experienced this week?

_____

_____

_____

3 STEPS WHEN DEALING WITH LOSS

1. Identify losses: What have you lost because of your parents' divorce?

_____

_____

_____

2. Accept and acknowledge losses: How have you accepted and acknowledged loss?

_____

_____

_____

3. Put losses in perspective: What is God's perspective in all of this?

_____

_____

_____

PRAYER REQUEST & PRAISE REPORTS

Write down prayer requests in the space provided and pray for one another during the week.

Stand firm
in this grace
& you will be
unshakable

Based on 1 Peter 5:9-12

CLOSING PRAYER

Dear God,

I need your comfort today. Thank you for being compassionate when I am hurting. Fill me with your joy and the peace of your Spirit. Direct my heart and mind toward you. Thank you for the reminder that both in seasons of celebration and in seasons of brokenness, you are still with me. For you will never leave me. Thank you that I am safe in your care. Please help me process my emotions and bring them to you. In Jesus' name. Amen.

Praise be to the
Father of Compassion
and the God of all
Comfort
who comforts us in all
our troubles,
so that we can
comfort those in
Any trouble.
2 Cor. 1:3-4

Look how far you have come! You have acknowledged your grief and sadness and have discovered new coping skills to process those emotions. Way to go. In the next lesson we discuss anger. Whether you think its relevant to your situation or not, you may learn something new that will help you help someone else.

GET THIS 2.0

9 Strategies to Overcome Sadness

Discuss as a group how these strategies could apply to your life. Write notes by the ones that most relate to your situation and how you want to take action steps this week.

Take care of your physical health:	**Connect with others:**
_____	_____
Don't dwell on negative thoughts:	**Begin helping or serving others:**
_____	_____
Find an accountability partner:	**Talk to a professional counselor:**
_____	_____
Eliminate untrue beliefs:	**Forgive people who have hurt you:**
_____	_____
Don't dismiss your true feelings:	
_____	

CHAPTER 7

Why Am I So Angry?

JACK'S STORY

"I hated my life. I hated it when I woke up and I hated it until I went to bed at night. It was such a dark place and I never knew I could find the support and hope I needed to feel better. My dad was an alcoholic and abused my mother, myself, and my siblings.

"I was relieved he left when I was twelve years old. My mom had to work two jobs to provide for us. We never had enough food to feed all five of us. I was horrible at school and finally dropped out to join the military. I eventually got my GED and started a new life away from all my family drama. After making many bad decisions, I hit rock bottom and turned to God for help.

"Eventually I turned my life around when I started to attend church. I found role models to show me what healthy relationships looked like and I admired the good families I observed. The church took me in and helped me find value in serving others. I've learned to control my anger and turn to God for help with my temper."

In your **ANGER**
Do not sin.
Do not let the sun go down
The sun go **DOWN**
While you are still **ANGRY.**
Eph. 4:26

ANGER IS NORMAL

It is normal to feel anger when your parents are separated or divorced. You may feel so angry with your parents that you can barely look at them without fury welling up inside. Knowing you would get in trouble if you screamed at your parents, you may try to hold the anger inside. You have the right to feel and express your true emotions, but we want to help you learn how to express them safely. To keep yourself and others protected, it is important to learn how to express your anger in healthy and appropriate ways.

Let's define what anger is first.

USE THESE WORDS TO FILL IN THE BLANKS.	
feeling	symptom
health	peace
God	serious
quickly	wrong

1. Anger is a person's response to a perceived _____.

2. Anger is a result of a person's judgements concerning _____, self, and others.

3. Anger involves a _____ of intense emotional displeasure.

4. Anger is not bad or sinful, it's what we do with that anger that can lead to a _____ problem.

The Lord is my **Strength** & **Shield** *I trust Him* with all my **Heart** *He helps me* & **My Heart** is filled with *Joy* Psalm 28:7

Clothe yourself with *Compassion* **Kindness** Humility GENTLENESS & PATIENCE COL. 3:12

5. Anger is a _____. It is an indication that something is wrong. You are frustrated. Disappointed. Hurt. Anger can lead to hate, bitterness, revenge, depression.

6. Anger lies underneath but it is the root that can steal your joy and _____ in your life.

7. It can grow _____.

8. Get your anger under control or it can destroy your physical and emotional _____.

A good man brings good things out of the good stored up in his heart, and an evil man brings evil things out of the evil stored up in his heart. For the mouth speaks what the heart is full of.

—Luke 6:45 NIV

A perceived wrong means you think someone owes you something like the truth or an apology. Do you feel like someone has wronged you or someone owes you?

_____

_____

_____

What do you think the difference is between being angry and being mad?

_____

_____

_____

Do not Grieve for the JOY of the Lord is your Strength!

Neh. 8.10

Do you think there is a difference between being happy and feeling joy?

_____

_____

_____

I once heard that happiness is based on something happening externally. Joy comes from within and is not based on circumstances. We can go through trials and challenges but still have the joy of the Lord inside us. We may not be happy with what we are going through, but Nehemiah 8:10 says, "For the joy of the Lord is your strength."

What does Nehemiah 8:10 mean to you?

_____

_____

_____

REJECTION

Your parents did not divorce you, but it may feel like you have been rejected and abandoned by one or both of them for breaking up your family. We must take the loss and hurt very seriously. Your parents may be full of rage over the divorce. Their personalities may be changing because anger has taken over their emotions. They may be acting out of this emotion, taking it out on you when you are not the one they are truly angry with.

Animals fight when they feel threatened and they need to defend and protect themselves. Angry people fight when they feel threatened, too. Now that your parents have split, they no longer have each other to fight with, but they still have this fury building up inside them. Sometimes that anger is directed at you just because you are there.

How can you relate this in your family?

_____

_____

_____

Anger can be triggered when you feel out of control. When others are trying to make decisions that affect you, but you have no control over it. You have every right to feel angry.

Describe how you usually express your feelings of anger.

_____

_____

_____

As a teenager, this is the time in your life that you are trying to gain more control, freedom, and independence from your parents. Parents are supposed to learn to let go of control during your teenage years and gradually trust you with more and more responsibility. Driving a car and starting a job to make your own money are part of growing up and gaining responsibility. In a healthy family, this transition is smooth and easy, but unfortunately, in most families, it's messy and challenging.

You may be angry at one or both of your parents because of the divorce. Out of anger you lash out because your life is out of control. The pain of divorce is causing anger to be revealed to the point that it seems like it has taken over the home. The only way to communicate is through fighting, but no one is winning.

Anger can offer a way to hide your fears and insecurity. But it's also a part of being out of control. Loneliness can trigger your anger. You can be separated from a favorite pet, a sibling, or grandparents.

What triggers your anger?

_____

_____

_____

Inferiority may also trigger anger—you may feel less worthy of love. Stuffing and suppressing angry feelings that grow inside of you can eventually explode. On the surface, you may say, "I'm fine," but you don't really mean it.

What have you said in the past to hide the fact that you are angry?

_____

_____

_____

Have you thought about talking honestly with God?

Don't deny your anger. Call it out and share it with God. Be angry but sin not. Go ahead and feel your emotions.

Did you know there's two types of aggressiveness? Passive aggression and open aggression.

Open aggression may involve throwing rocks, scratching a car, or hurting someone else. An alternative suggestion is to kick empty boxes to physically release your anger, or get a punching bag, exercise, or go for a run.

Passive aggression is more like giving the silent treatment, walking away to another room, emotionally separating from your parents. Shutting away in your room.

Escaping by watching TV or playing video games. Pulling away and hiding from the source of your anger. Refusing to be cooperative, not helping with chores, not following through with what is expected of you. Procrastinating with school assignments. Not feeling like studying for tests.

How have you acted out with passive aggression?

_____

_____

_____

Get rid of All **Bitterness** RAGE & ANGER & **Brawling** & **Slander** along with every form of MALICE. Be Kind & **Compassionate** & to one another, **Forgiving** Each other, just as God through Christ has forgiven you
Eph. 4:31-32

Ephesians 4:31–32 NIV says, *"Get rid of all bitterness, rage and anger, brawling and slander, along with every form of malice. Be kind and compassionate to one another, forgiving each other, just as in Christ God forgave you."*

Admit you are angry. Stop denying it. You can't work on anger until you acknowledge you have a problem with anger.

TAKE INVENTORY

· ·

When you feel angry, here are some questions to help you process your anger by helping you determine the cause.

- Why do I feel angry?
- Who am I angry with?
- Why am I angry at them?

- Am I angry at myself?
- What is productive about this anger?
- What do I do with this anger?

5 TIPS FOR DEALING WITH ANGER

· ·

Your broken family stirs up many deep emotions, perhaps even some you've never experienced before. Riding out these painful feelings is about the most important thing you can do.

USE THESE WORDS TO FILL IN THE BLANKS.	
Calm Hear Relax	Safe Slow

1. It's important to vent your feelings in a _____ place.

2. Talking with someone helps by reflecting your feelings so you can literally _____ it spoken back to you.

3. Find ways to _____ and release the tension in your body. Get into a calm position. Take deep breaths. Count to ten.

4. Aggressive angry behavior does not _____ you down.

5. Take a time out. _____ down. Don't speak impulsively. You can't be tense and relaxed at the same time. Chill out. You could say, "I am too angry to talk to you right now. I'm going to take 20 minutes to cool down, pray, and meditate."

Here is a good verse to have on your mirror during your cool down period: *And now, dear brothers and sisters, one final thing. Fix your thoughts on what is true, and honorable, and right, and pure, and lovely, and admirable. Think about things that are excellent and worthy of praise* (Philippians 4:8).

Turn to God. He will understand and reveal why you are angry.

What are you trying to control?

What do you need to surrender to God's control?

He can change your circumstances, or He can change you!

Fix your thoughts
On what is true
& honorable
RIGHT &
PURE
Lovely &
Admirable.
Think about things that are
Excellent &
Worthy of Praise
Phil. 4:8

IN OTHER WORDS...

66 It's not going to be easy but they need to find comfort in something they love to do. Also they should know that no matter what they are loved. It's hard going through something that you feel so lonely in and having that type of love whether it's from the one parent or just a family member, it's truly needed to have that support in dealing with the divorce."

—*Kora, 16*

PRAYER REQUEST **&** PRAISE REPORTS

Write down prayer requests in the space provided and pray for one another during the week.

I know the Lord is always with me. I will not be **Shaken** for he is Right beside me.

Psalm 16:8

CLOSING PRAYER

Dear God,

I have to face my anger and it scares me. Help me let go of anger, bitterness, rage and frustration. I want to trust you with all my heart. I pray you will be my strength when I feel weak and frustrated with my family. Holy Spirit please reveal to me what I am angry about

The Lord is close to the brokenhearted & Rescues those whose Spirits are crushed.

Psalm 34:18

and help me confess and repent of it. I do not want to respond in anger towards others who may have hurt me. Help me see a way out of this feeling. Please take my pain away and replace it with your joy. Even if the circumstances don't change, you can change me. I pray for your peace to help me let go. In Jesus' name. Amen.

Next week we will continue our discussion on anger to learn even more ways to deal with it for our health and benefit.

Facing Your Anger

In the left column, make a list of things that you are angry about regarding your parents' divorce. Number them in order from those that make you feel the angriest to those that make you the least upset.

In the right column, describe actions you can take that are safe and appropriate ways to express anger.

Talk with a counselor or other adult about how you can put these ideas into practice.

What are you angry about?	List actions you can take to express the anger

CHAPTER 8

How do I Deal with Anger?

NICK'S STORY

"I was so angry about my parents' divorce that I could barely look at them without feeling rage inside of me. I knew I would get into trouble if I expressed it by screaming at them, so I held it in at home the best I could. One day after my mom left for work, I went to my room and slammed my fist through my bedroom wall. At school, I started getting into fights with anyone who irritated me. The slightest thing would set me off and I just didn't know how else to respond. I let my fist do the talking for me. After three fights I was suspended.

"My mom took me to a counselor to talk about my feelings. It was the last place I wanted to be. After a while I started to open up to the counselor and realized there were healthier ways to deal with my anger. He didn't judge me or make me feel weak for needing help. He was a good listener and only gave advice when I asked for it. He helped me find my own answers my own way and I liked that he treated me with respect."

Get rid of All
Bitterness
RAGE &
ANGER &
Brawling
& Slander
along with every form of
MALICE.
Eph. 4:31

HEALTHY WAYS OF DEALING WITH ANGER

USE THESE WORDS TO FILL IN THE BLANKS.	
Learn	Listen
Cause	God
Bible	Out
Anger	Relax

1. Acknowledge and be aware of your _____

2. Find ways to _____

3. Determine the _____

4. Take a time _____

5. Find someone to _____

6. Give it to _____

7. Read your _____

8. _____ and practice response strategies

From the list above, which ones do you think you are able to do already? Which ones do you want to work on?

MANAGING ANGER IS A PROCESS

• •

The Bible has some good suggestions on how to bring your anger under control and how to diffuse explosive situations:

"A gentle answer deflects anger, but harsh words make tempers flare" (Proverbs 15:1).

USE THESE WORDS TO FILL IN THE BLANKS.	
others	fix
more	voice
a gentle answer	slowly
age	listen
harsh words	handle

1. What is a suggested solution to handle anger based on Proverbs 15?

   _____

2. According to this Bible verse, what causes anger to flare?

   _____

   How you say things, your tone, is just as important as what you say. Have you ever been misunderstood because of the tone of your voice? _____

   Timing is everything, too. Have you approached someone who was busy and distracted and the conversation didn't go as expected? Be aware of the timing when you approach certain topics. _____

   Can you share an example when your timing was off or when someone approached you and their timing was wrong?

   _____

   _____

   _____

3. Learn to respond to _____ in healthy ways.

4. Don't escalate the anger and provoke others to _____ anger.

5. Speak in a calm _____.

6. Speak _____.

7. Sometimes people just want you to _____. They just want to be heard.

8. You don't have to _____ their problems. Take it to the Lord.

9. Parents dump on you because you are there. They don't hesitate to think about your _____ and your maturity level.

10. They may dump more on you than you can _____.

An angry or bitter spirit will draw people away from you. Friends will not want to hang out with you if you are filled with anger.

Christ will help you make amends with those you have hurt in your anger. Apologize and change your ways. Don't just say sorry and continue doing the same thing over and over again. God will help you change the more you submit to His Holy Spirit living inside of you. You can react in a peaceful way with more of Christ controlling your life.

The Bible has some good suggestions on how to bring your anger under control and how to diffuse explosive situations:

Ecclesiastes 7:9 says, "Control your temper, for anger labels you a fool."

This suggests that you not allow yourself to become quickly provoked. Discuss some ideas on how you might avoid quickly reacting in anger.

Control your TEMPER for Anger Labels you a FOOL.
Ecc. 7:9

Where do you get the power to resist acting out in anger?

_____

_____

_____

CAN GOD HELP ME CONTROL MY ANGER?

• •

We've talked about the importance of having a personal relationship with Christ to help in your healing. When you give control of your life to Him, the Bible says the Spirit of God comes to live inside you.

Read Galatians 5:19–26. *When you follow the desires of your sinful nature, the results are very clear: sexual immorality, impurity, lustful pleasures, idolatry, sorcery, hostility, quarreling, jealousy, outbursts of anger, selfish ambition, dissension, division, envy, drunkenness, wild parties, and other sins like these. Let me tell you again, as I have before, that anyone living that sort of life will not inherit the Kingdom of God. But the Holy Spirit produces this kind of fruit in our lives: love, joy, peace, patience, kindness, goodness, faithfulness, gentleness, and self-control. There is no law against these things. Those who belong to Christ Jesus have nailed the passions and desires of their sinful nature to his cross and crucified them there. Since we are living by the Spirit, let us follow the Spirit's leading in every part of our lives. Let us not become conceited, or provoke one another, or be jealous of one another.*

What type of life will you live if you don't have God's Spirit in you?

_____

_____

_____

What are the indicators that you have God's Spirit in your life?

_____

_____

_____

Have you invited Christ into your life? Yes or No

Is the Holy Spirit evident in your life? Yes or No

The Holy Spirit produces this kind of fruit in our lives: Love, Joy, PEACE, Patience, Kindness, Goodness, Faithfulness, Gentleness, & Self-control. Gal. 5:22-23

According to Galatians 5:22–23, which of the qualities listed would you like more of in your life?

_____

_____

_____

If you are a Christian and have the Holy Spirit living inside you, then you have all of the fruits (characteristics) of the Spirit. How evident these characteristics are in your life depends on how yielded you are to the Holy Spirit.

Read John 15:5.

I am the VINE You are the BRANCHES he who abides in Me & I in him will bear much FRUIT John 15:5

Living by faith begins with admitting that we can do nothing apart from God.

What does it look like to abide in God?

3 WAYS TO DEAL WITH ANGER

Handling anger is an important topic. Anger is so commonplace that we often accept it as the normal. Practically every day we see people getting angry. Counselors report that 50% of people who come in for counseling have problems dealing with anger. Did you know that over 60% of people lose their tempers at least once a week?

Anger likes to hide, be buried, or covered up. Sometimes we're not even aware it's there. But anger that's stuffed away won't remain hidden forever. When it breaks out, it may catch us by surprise.

We can overcome extreme bitterness in our heart that resulted from being hurt or betrayed. Here are 3 ways to begin looking at anger differently and handling it in a way that pleases God.

1. Don't keep it all inside–talk it out. The longer we hold our anger in, the more agitated it can become, so when it erupts, the outcome will always be ugly. Talk to God about your feelings and talk to someone you trust who can support you in your desire to let your anger go.

2. If you can't change the person or circumstance which angered you, change yourself. Anyone can return evil for evil, but it takes a courageous person to allow love to flow from their heart instead of hatred. Even if your mind wants to take revenge, talk to God about helping you have the willpower to offer forgiveness. It might not change the external problem, but it will change your internal ability to handle the situation.

3. Remember that no matter how justified we feel in our anger; no matter how hopeless a situation seems; and no matter how aggravating a situation may be— God is always there. He helps us deal with our anger in the right way.

Compare these two versions of a verse from the New Testament when Paul wrote the Corinthians.

No test or temptation that comes your way is beyond the course of what others have had to face. All you need to remember is that God will never let you down; he'll never let you be pushed past your limit; he'll always be there to help you come through it (1 Corinthians 10:13 The Message).

The temptations in your life are no different from what others experience. And God is faithful. He will not allow the temptation to be more than you can stand. When you are tempted, he will show you a way out so that you can endure (1 Corinthians 10:13).

How would you write this verse in your own words?

_____

_____

_____

_____

_____

_____

PRAYER REQUEST & PRAISE REPORTS

Write down prayer requests in the space provided and pray for one another during the week.

Stand firm
in this grace
& you will be
unshakable
Based on 1 Peter 5:9-12

CLOSING PRAYER

Dear God,

Help me to rest in the truth of Psalm 86:13 that says, "Great is your love toward me." You already see the ways I will fall short and mess up. But right now, I receive your

Then you called out to God
in your *desperate* condition.
He got you out in the nick of time.
He spoke the word
that *healed* you.
Psalm 107:19

unconditional love for me. I recognize Your love for me is not based on my behavior. I'm sorry I get angry at times and really want to change. God please show me when I am angered and help me deal with it in healthy ways, so I don't hurt myself or others. Thank you that you love me in spite of my anger and frustration. That's amazing. But what's more amazing is that Jesus wants a relationship with me. God, I want to believe. If there is any unbelief in me, take it away. In Jesus' name. Amen.

Now that we have learned about anger and its power to cause problems, next week we will discuss forgiveness. There are times we need to forgive and times when we need to be forgiven from others, too.

GET THIS 2.0

What Are My Rights?

LOVE BOTH PARENTS

You have the right to love BOTH parents.

Sometimes during a divorce, one parent is so angry or hurt that they try to encourage you to turn away from the other parent and remain loyal only to them. No matter what happens between your parents, you have the right to love both of them and to remain equally loyal.

Discuss if you have been put in a position to choose one parent over the other.

If you feel anxious about sharing your rights to either of your parents, you might try one or all of these suggestions to help make things easier:

1. Rehearse what you will say beforehand, either by yourself or with someone else.

2. Ask another adult you trust to be present with you when you talk to your parents.

3. Talk to your parents in a counselor's office to help your family communicate clearly and peacefully.

You have the right to remain separate from your parents' problems.

The problems in their relationship are their responsibility, not yours. Some parents may try to draw you into their drama and get you in the middle of it, but that is not fair to you or appropriate behavior.

Describe how it would feel for you to tell your parents to stop putting you in the middle of their problems.

You have the right to remain a teenager.

When parents divorce and then live without an adult partner, they may begin to treat you as another adult instead of their child. This puts you in a new role that you are not ready to take on at your age. This is not fair to you. You have the right to remain in a child's role in your relationship with your parents.

- Have you been told you are the "Man of the House" now that your father has left the home?
- Are you having to care for your siblings by preparing meals, laundry, and rides?
- Are you lending money to help pay bills?

While it's fine to help with babysitting or doing chores around the house occasionally, it is not your job to take on parental duties. Parents do not need to treat their teens as peers and divulge adult problems and issues. Adults need to find adult friends to share their lives with in a healthy, social, and relational way.

Describe a situation where your mom or dad may have put you in the role of an adult.

_____

_____

_____

Explain how this made you feel and why.

_____

_____

_____

Write how you could help your parents understand how you feel and suggest ways that they could find an alternative approach to meeting their needs.

_____

_____

_____

YOU HAVE THE RIGHT TO BE PARENTED.

Sometimes when parents get divorced, they become self-absorbed in their own lives and neglect some of their parental duties. No matter what is happening in their lives, you have the right to be provided with adequate care from both of your parents.

- Have you had enough groceries in your home?
- How often do you have to make your own meals?
- Do you have someone to help you with your homework?
- Do you have a parent come to your athletic games or dance recitals?
- Do you have reliable transportation to and from school and school related events?

- Do you have a parent available for doctor's office visits, dentists, and when other medical needs arise?
- Do you have internet and computer access at home to complete your schoolwork?
- What kinds of things do you do on the weekends with your mom?
- What kinds of things do you do on the weekends with your dad?

OTHER RIGHTS YOU HAVE

- You have the right to stay connected with extended family on both sides.
- You have the right to be treated with respect from all family members.
- You have the right to share your opinion when making decisions that affect the family.

- You have the right to share your feelings.
- You have the right to ask for help from a trusted adult or counselor.

CHAPTER 9

How Do I Forgive Others?

"My dad made sure his new wife and her daughter had more than they needed, while my brother and I felt like beggars asking him to help our mom with basic things. Every cheeseburger, item of clothing, or activity came with a reminder of "what they spent on us." As we became teenagers, she would sometimes send us bills for expenses. As children, it was clear we were a burden to her. She mocked me for my faith, and I was often referred to as "little Miss Perfect" or "just like my mom." It was clear she was jealous that my dad gave anything to us, including love.

"When my dad was diagnosed with Alzheimer's at the age of 53, my stepmom took the best care of him. During his final years, God was orchestrating a series of unique events that set up a powerful story of forgiveness and restoration. After spending time with Dad each week, she began to see me for who I really am, a person who longed to have a relationship with her, and in no way, a threat. We talked about faith and I watched her be the best caregiver to my dad I could have imagined. The same woman who said often, "I'm not your maid," selflessly became my dad's everything. God had changed her before my very eyes, and I got to witness it. Even now, I have the gift of an ongoing relationship with her—we remember my dad together, and I see the beautiful person God made her to be.

"Not every broken relationship has a happy ending on earth. But I know that God desires restoration more than we do. We are often put into families we do not choose. If we will listen to Him, He will guide us and give us what we need.

"When our families are broken, God grieves with us. He often wants to show us that His ways are better than ours. Forgiveness for our mistakes and our family's messes are possible through Him."

You must be compassionate just as your Father is Compassionate.

Luke 6:36

FORGIVE? NO WAY!

Our typical reaction when we've been hurt badly is self-protection, which means a resistance to forgive. When parents divorce, you may find yourself wanting to blame one parent or the other for the split. It can feel easier to label one parent the "bad guy" and one parent the "good guy." But neither parent is all good or all bad. Accepting that one parent has both positive and negative traits can be uncomfortable or confusing.

Do you have trouble seeing both parents as having a part in breaking up the family?

There may be several factors that contributed to the separation or divorce.

Write down any factors that may have led to your family's breakup.

_____

_____

_____

Instead of placing blame on a person, what would it look like to focus on letting go of the bitterness and anger you may have been holding onto since this difficult situation started?

Why do you think God wants us to forgive others?

What if the other person doesn't deserve to be forgiven? This week we will discuss the answers to these questions and more.

Choosing not to forgive is choosing bitterness. It is choosing to be connected to the person who wronged you. Negative feelings are valid, but they must be dealt with, so they won't cause problems in your future. When we conceal our anger, sadness, and fear, it results in depression, anxiety, and grudges in our relationships.

> ## If you are choosing to withhold forgiveness, how do you think it is affecting you?

Forgiveness is not forgetting. With time, you will not hurt as much because you learned to let go and forgive. People don't heal in order to forgive—they forgive in order to heal. Forgiveness comes first.

Forgiveness is a choice, a decision of the will. Since God requires you to forgive, it is something you can do with God's help.

Some people hold onto their anger as a means of protecting themselves against further pain, but all they are doing is hurting themselves. When you don't forgive, you are chained to your past, bound up in your bitterness.

By forgiving, you let the other person go and let God take care of them. The Bible teaches in Romans 12:19, "Dear friends, never take revenge. Leave that to the righteous anger of God. For the Scriptures say, 'I will take revenge; I will pay them back,' says the Lord."

What do you think Romans 12:19 is telling you to do?

_____

_____

_____

You may be thinking, *but you don't know how much this person hurt me.* No other human really knows another person's pain, but Jesus does. He instructs us to forgive others for our own sake. Until you let go of your bitterness and hate, the person who caused your wounds is still hurting you. We are to forgive as Christ has forgiven us.

Forgive from your heart. Allow God to bring your painful memories to the surface and acknowledge how you feel toward those who've hurt you. If your forgiveness doesn't touch the emotional core of your life, it will be incomplete. Too often we are afraid of the pain, so we bury our emotions deep down inside us. Let God bring them to the surface so He can begin to heal those painful memories.

From Paul's letter to the Ephesians, what is he asking them to get rid of from Ephesians 4:31–32?

BE KIND TO EACH OTHER, *tenderhearted* FORGIVING ONE ANOTHER *just ast God through* CHRIST HAS FORGIVEN YOU.
EPH. 4:32

According to this verse, why should we forgive one another?

_____

_____

_____

When we understand how much we have been forgiven, we can extend forgiveness to those who have deeply hurt us.

What action step is God asking of you today based on Ephesians 4?

_____

_____

_____

Let's look at what forgiveness really is.

FORGIVENESS

••

USE THESE WORDS TO FILL IN THE BLANKS.	
lead control God's process gift debt revenge	good trust enabling forgetting apology sin covering

1. Forgiveness is canceling a _____ owed to you.

2. Forgiveness is removing the _____ the offender has over you.

3. Forgiveness is giving a _____ to yourself and to your offender.

4. Forgiveness is not taking _____.

5. Forgiveness is leaving the ultimate justice in _____ hands.

6. Forgiveness is an ongoing _____.

7. Forgiveness is wanting _____ for your offender.

8. Forgiveness is not denying that _____ occurred or diminishing its wrong.

9. Forgiveness is not _____.

10. Forgiveness is not just accepting an _____.

11. Forgiveness is not _____ up crimes that were committed against us.

12. Forgiveness is not _____.

13. Forgiveness is not _____.

14. Forgiveness is not reconciliation, but it can _____ to it.

66 If we see ourselves as all good, and this totally righteous, pure heart, then we won't be as apt to offer forgiveness. We really need to see ourselves in our true state, desperately in need of forgiveness, and then in turn, understand and have compassion on other people who need it too."

—GEORGIA SHAFFER

WHAT IF I DON'T FEEL LIKE FORGIVING?

Make the hard choice to forgive even if you don't feel like it. Once you choose to forgive, God will begin to heal your damaged heart.

Don't pray, "*Lord, help me to forgive.*" God is already helping you.

Don't pray, "*Lord, I want to forgive.*" Because that bypasses the hard choice you have to make.

Instead pray, "*Lord, I choose to forgive* _____ *for what they did to me.*" When you pray explain what they did to hurt you. Talk openly to God about how it made you feel and be specific. This is part of the healing process.

If you forgive those who sin **against you,** Your Heavenly Father **will forgive you.** Matt. 6:14

But when you are praying, first forgive anyone you are holding **a grudge against, so that** Your Father in heaven will **Forgive your sins, too.** Mark 11:25

Matthew and Mark were close friends of Jesus and wrote these verses for us to learn about forgiveness.

> **What do these verses have in common?**

WRITE YOUR OWN LETTER

Ask the Holy Spirit to help you by bringing people to your mind and make a list of the names of people you need to forgive. You may be mad at your parents for fighting and splitting up the family. You may be angry at a sibling or another family member for hurting you or for not being there for you when you needed them. When our needs are not met, we blame people for not meeting our expectations. Forgiving them is a step towards healing.

This may sound strange, but add your name to the list, too. Write your name at the bottom of your list if you need to forgive yourself.

Why would you need to forgive yourself? Guilt and anger towards ourselves can add to the pain we feel. In order to release that pain, you have to let the past go and forgive yourself for any mistakes you have made.

Also write down, *Thoughts Against God* on your list. Obviously, God has never done anything wrong, so He doesn't need our forgiveness. But we need to let go of our disappointments with our Heavenly Father. Maybe you prayed for your parents not to get divorced and God didn't answer your prayer. People hold on to angry thoughts because God did not do what they wanted Him to do. Those feelings of anger or resentment toward God need to be released.

It is very common to become angry at God because of your family situation. Asking God:

- *"How could You let this happen?"*
- *"Why weren't You there?"*
- *"If you are in control of everything, why didn't You answer my prayers?"*

These are all normal questions and feelings to have. People are often afraid to admit their anger towards God, because they are afraid He will punish them. We tend to hide this anger toward God because we are ashamed to tell anyone. Let me assure you, it's okay to be angry with God. In the entire universe, God is the only one able to absorb your anger. No matter how mad you are at God, His loving arms are waiting to embrace you.

Sometimes, we need to forgive others, sometimes ourselves, and sometimes even God, because we blame Him for our circumstances. Write a letter that may or may not be given to anyone. Then tear it up and throw it away. When you get your feelings out, pray out loud and let God heal your heart and set you free from all bitterness and anger.

ROB'S STORY

Recognizing, accepting, and expressing anger can be a very healing experience. I know a young man who endured a lot of verbal abuse from his father growing up. When his father died, the man had a difficult time dealing with his pent-up anger. Finally, he wrote a long letter to his father describing all his painful memories and angry feelings. He went to his father's grave and read the letter aloud. He felt self-conscious at first, but soon his emotions took over and he was able to get his anger out. As he knelt at his father's grave, the tears flowed, and years of hurt and anger were washed away.

A PRAYER OF FORGIVENESS

Praying out loud releases our burdens and helps us find the freedom and healing we need, so we can move forward. Here is a suggested prayer to help guide you to release those who you need to forgive. Practice using this prayer whenever the need comes up for a variety of different people and situations.

Dear Heavenly Father,

I choose to forgive _____ for _____, because it made me feel____.

After you have forgiven that person for every painful memory, then pray as follows.

Lord Jesus,

I choose not to hold on to my resentment. I choose not to hold any of these things against _____any longer. I thank you for setting me free from the bondage of my bitterness toward _____. I ask you to heal my damaged emotions. I now ask you to bless _____in Jesus' name, I pray. Amen.

If the word "bitterness" does not fit how you feel about that person, then pick a different word that is a better fit for your circumstances. One girl I met with, replaced bitterness with the word "sadness," and when she was free from the bondage of sadness over her parents' divorce, a huge weight lifted off her shoulders. Her face lit up with a smile I had never seen before.

Take time tonight or this week when you are on your own to pray this prayer out loud, filling in the blanks with the names from your list and the details of your situation. This should be done in private, so you feel safe. God's presence will be with you to help you through this exercise.

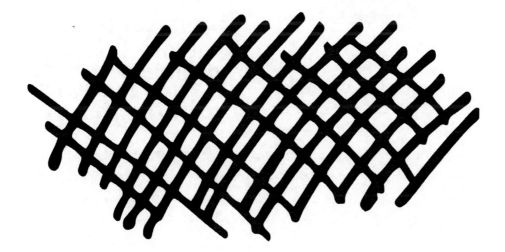

PRAYER REQUEST & PRAISE REPORTS

Write down prayer requests in the space provided and pray for one another during the week.

I know the Lord is always with me. I will not be **Shaken** for he is Right beside me.

Psalm 16:8

CLOSING PRAYER

Dear God,

If there is anyone I need to forgive, please show me and help me to forgive them. It's hard to let go of hurts. I am sorry for blaming others for causing my pain. I need your help to let go. Lord, I don't want anything to separate me from obeying your will for my life. Teach me how to choose only your way so that I can continue on this path of healing. Help me walk in your peace and help me not let my feelings control me. Protect me from my own careless thoughts, words, and actions. I want to receive your forgiveness just as much as I want to forgive others. In Jesus' name. Amen.

If you forgive those who sin **against you,** Your Heavenly Father **will forgive you.**

Matt. 6:14

Forgiveness is a key step to restore relationships and build trust. Another important element you need is the communication skills that aide in conflict resolution. Every family has some conflict to deal with, even when divorce isn't an issue. These practical tools will equip you for real life situations, in and outside your home.

The next lesson will provide practical tools to equip you for real life situations, in and outside your home.

What's Behind the Anger?

FEELING NEGLECTED OR ABANDONED?

You may feel a sense of abandonment from your parents' divorce, because their attention is spread thin with all the challenges the family is facing. You may feel like you lost the security and predictable life you once had.

During your teenage years, you are learning to become more independent, and in a way, separate from dependence on your parents. When parents divorce, however, you may feel like they have separated from you. You may feel a sense of abandonment.

Have you felt neglected or left on your own to take care of yourself?

_____

_____

_____

_____

_____

How has that made you feel?

_____

_____

_____

_____

_____

4 TIPS TO HELP YOU COPE

• •

Here are a few suggestions to help you deal with your feelings of abandonment or neglect.

- Tell your mom and dad how you feel. Let them reassure you of their love and spend regular time with each one of them. (One family started daddy/daughter dates as a way to connect and focus on their relationship. Mothers and sons need to find things they enjoy together, too.)

- Stay close to your extended family. Your connection with your grandparents, aunts, uncles, cousins, and family friends will give you the security you may feel is missing.

- Stay in touch with other adults you feel close to, like a teacher, coach, neighbor, spiritual leader, or someone else. Remember, they are there to support you when you need someone new to talk to.

- Continue to go out with your friends and participate in other social activities that you enjoy. Try new things and meet new people. You will build confidence in yourself and learn to trust others again gradually.

CHAPTER 10

How Can I Communicate & Handle Conflict

CORA'S STORY

Blended families don't always start out smoothly. Cora had to learn how to adapt to a new stepfather and stepbrother.

"There's certain things you love about someone that can drive you crazy. It hasn't been awful. When we first got to know Stan, he was shy. Stan and his son joked around a lot and they poked fun. My sister and I don't get sarcasm, so we didn't understand the way they joked around with each other.

"His son, Andy, lived with us during his senior year. We didn't get along, because we had to accommodate Andy and make him happy. Mom got upset when we didn't get along with each other. They wanted the family to be together all the time, but I didn't ever get to talk to my mom, she was always with Stan. It was hard to get her alone. She was always working and when she was home, she was around him. I didn't want to open up to her when he was around.

"On my day off, I was finally able to take my mom out to dinner to talk about how I was feeling. We made a pact to get together at least once a month for "mother/daughter time." This way we could have fun and chat about whatever we needed to without the guys around. This turned out to be a great solution, and I looked forward to our time together."

CHILDREN OBEY YOUR PARENTS
because you belong
to the Lord
for this is the
right thing to do.
Eph. 6:1

COMMUNICATION

In the middle of changing and adjusting to your parents' splitting up or divorcing, communication (talking to each other, especially about important things) can get even more difficult. Some families become so frustrated they give up trying and stop communicating for long periods of time. More and more families are spending time separated in every room around the house: playing videos, on their phones, watching TV, or streaming. When this happens, family members are not spending time together, which feels lonely and isolating, even when people are sharing the same home.

It's important to keep talking about your circumstances and how you feel. Right now, the divorce seems to monopolize everyone's attention and thoughts, but it's not the only thing going on in your life. Do everything you can, even when it's hard, to engage with your parents.

TALKING WITH YOUR PARENTS

Amelia thinks to herself, *I'm hurting inside.*

- What is Amelia feeling? _____
- What problem could result from Amelia not sharing her thoughts and feelings? _____
- What would you suggest Amelia say to her parents about how she feels?

Mark wonders, *Will I ever see my dad again?*

- What is Mark feeling? _____
- What problem could result from Mark not sharing his thoughts and feelings? _____
- What would you suggest Mark say to his parents about how he feels?

Sabrina wonders, *Is it my fault my parents got divorced?*

- What is Sabrina feeling? _____
- What problem could result from Sabrina not sharing her thoughts and feelings? _____
- What would you suggest Sabrina say to her parents about how she feels?

Daniel asks, *Why did my parents do this to me?*

- What is Daniel feeling? _____
- What problem could result from Daniel not sharing his thoughts and feelings? _____
- What would you suggest Daniel say to his parents about how he feels?

OPEN COMMUNICATION

Dealing with your parents splitting up involves open and honest communication. Many teenagers start to have a bad relationship with their parents because they stop talking. You have to commit to communicating with your parents about all kinds of stuff going on in your life, even when you don't feel like it.

When you feel angry or upset about your parents getting divorced, you may want to avoid both your feelings and your parents. However, communicating with them is a healthy way you can help relieve and release difficult feelings. Talking or writing letters about how you feel can be uncomfortable or even overwhelming. However, communicating could also help heal relationships between family members.

HOW DO I TALK ABOUT MY FEELINGS?

Let's discuss why you think it can be hard to talk about your feelings with your parents.

USE THESE WORDS TO FILL IN THE BLANKS.

safe

problems

share

happen

plan

---

1. _____ any thoughts or feelings you have that you are worried about sharing with your parents.

2. What do you think might _____ if you shared these thoughts and feelings with your parents?

3. Describe any _____ that are happening because you are not communicating with your parents.

4. What would you say to your parents if you felt _____ enough to do so?

5. Make a _____ to communicate with your parents when you feel most comfortable doing so.

WHAT DOES THE BIBLE SAY ABOUT IT?

HONOR YOUR FATHER & MOTHER *As the Lord your God* COMMANDED YOU *Then you will live a long,* FULL LIFE IN THE LAND THE *Lord your God* IS GIVING YOU.
Deut.5:16

CHILDREN OBEY YOUR PARENTS **because you belong** *to the Lord* for this is the **right thing to do.**
Eph.6:1

What do the verses above tell you to do in regard to your parents?

_____

_____

_____

How can you show honor to your parents? What does that look like?

_____

_____

_____

HOW TO HANDLE CONFLICT

Transitioning to a new family can be a really big adjustment. It may not be easy and could bring unique challenges. While everybody is getting used to each other, you can count on a few tense moments. Over time, your new family living situation will become more comfortable. Handling conflict does not have to be stressful and add more drama to your life.

You may wish you could avoid conflict and pray for peace in your home, but no matter how much you pray, people are going to lose their patience with one another. Human beings are imperfect. Families, roommates, co-workers, friends, even animals have conflict. It's part of life.

> **How can we communicate with each other in a way that does not make the other person feel threatened?**

When we feel attacked, we get defensive. That's where conflict gets uncomfortable!

Let's learn some practical ways to communicate, so we can decrease the amount of conflict whenever possible.

After filling in the words, put a (+) by the ones you already use and a (-) by those you might need to work on.

TIPS TO DECREASE CONFLICT

USE THESE WORDS TO FILL IN THE BLANKS.	
out	topic
respond	should
you	focus
always	positive
avoid	body
threats	attention
name	good

1. Stop using the words "never" and _____.

2. Avoid blame, shame or _____calling.

3. Use "I" statements rather than _____ statements.

4. Take a time_____ when needed.

5. Check out what you hear before you_____.

6. _____ interrupting.

7. Avoid using _____.

8. Be _____.

9. _____ on one problem or concern.

10. If you're really nervous, test the waters first with a less threatening _____.

11. Pay attention to your _____ language.

12. Pay _____ to their body language, too.

13. Avoid using the word _____.

14. Choose a time that's _____ for both of you.

A BUG AND A WISH

Here's a fun way to address things that are bothering you without it escalating into a huge conflict. Your family could implement this technique at the dinner table each night to nip tension in the bud before it grows into a bigger problem.

Try using this phrase when you need to get something off your chest.

"It bugs me when _____, and I wish you would _____ instead."

By using this phrase, you are expressing what irritates you, and can offer a solution to the problem. Others can respond by offering a different solution, and you can negotiate action you both agree upon.

Here are some examples:

• It bugs me when <u>you put onions and peppers in the salad,</u> and I wish you would <u>leave them on the side</u> instead.

• It bugs me when <u>I have to ask you to come to the dinner table 10 times,</u> and I wish you would <u>turn off your phone and come to the table the first time I ask.</u>

- It bugs me when you <u>go to the grocery store and don't ask me what I want for lunches,</u> and I wish you would <u>ask me once a week and buy a few things I like instead.</u>

- It bugs me when <u>you make me babysit my siblings every night,</u> and I wish you would <u>let me have at least three nights off instead.</u>

- It bugs me when <u>you make me clean the kitchen every night when I'm not the one who makes the mess,</u> and <u>I wish everyone could clean up after themselves</u> instead.

What are some examples you could use for A Bug and a Wish?

_____

_____

_____

GETTING ALONG WITH FAMILY

During conflict, you may want so badly to be heard that you talk over others, or you think about your next statement when you're supposed to be listening. Proverbs 18:13 says, "Spouting off before listening to the facts is both shameful and foolish."

It takes great discipline but remember to listen first to understand the other person before trying to be understood. This will help the conflicts to decrease and lead to more productive conversations. You may be asking yourself, "Do I have to like them?"

What do you like about your current family?

_____

_____

_____

What do you wish could be better with your family members?

_____

_____

_____

There are going to be things about your family changes that you don't like, things that bug you, and things that are different than you are used to. But give them a chance. Different is not always a bad thing.

DON'T SHUT DOWN

When you feel like you are not in control, it's tempting to sit back and stay silent. You may stay quiet because you're angry or maybe because you don't think it's right to speak your mind. Your parents need to hear your thoughts and you need to share them. It's okay to feel angry, sad, hurt, and disappointed. It's okay to share those feelings with your parents. Their decisions involve you and affect you, too. If you can't talk to them, be sure to talk to someone else you trust. Bring an adult with you to help you have a positive conversation with your parents about what you are struggling with.

HONOR YOUR PARENTS

You may be upset about your parents' divorce, but you are still called to honor them. They are still your parents, and even though it's hard, you still need to try. Honoring them means showing respect to them whether you are in their presence or not. It's important to stay respectful when talking to others about your parents.

What are some other ways you can show respect to your parents?

_____

_____

_____

When you're feeling extreme emotions (like you either want to cry or throw things because you are so frustrated), get a bit of space to be by yourself, if possible.

If you're in the middle of a loud conversation with your siblings, ask them if it's okay that you take a few minutes by yourself to think. Go to your room and try to quiet yourself down. Count to 10 or 20 or 100,000.

What are some other coping skills you could try?

_____

_____

_____

Those who fear the Lord **are secure;** He will be a *refuge* **for their children.**
Prov. 14:26

(Pray and ask God to help you understand your family. Ask God to help them remain patient with you and try to understand your feelings, too.)

PRAYER REQUEST & PRAISE REPORTS

Write down prayer requests in the space provided and pray for one another during the week.

Stand firm
in this grace
& you will be
unshakable

Based on 1 Peter 5:9-12

CLOSING PRAYER

Dear God,

I need you. I need courage as I go through this day. I have to communicate tough things with my parents and I'm feeling afraid. Help me put my thoughts together so I can clearly communicate with them in a way they will hear and understand. Guide me to safe adults like a counselor, teacher, mentor, or friend who can go with me to talk to my parents. When I am tempted to give up, help me to keep going. Grant me a cheerful spirit if things don't go my way. Please give me courage to do whatever needs to be done. Help me gain a new perspective and find hope through my faith in you. In Jesus' name, Amen.

CHILDREN OBEY YOUR PARENTS **because you belong** *to the Lord* for this is the **right thing to do.**
Eph. 6:1

Try to use "A Bug and A Wish" this week and let us know how that goes next week. We will discuss more about family dynamics and how to adjust to the ever-increasing changes and challenges when families come together.

GET THIS 2.0

The Power of Attitude

Do you ever feel like you wake up in a different mood every morning? Does it seem like your feelings are all over the place at times? Did you know that your feelings come from your thoughts? You can actually control your own thoughts, which means you can control your feelings. Choosing to have positive thoughts and a positive attitude can help you cope with your parents' divorce. Let's look at how Sophia and David chose to think about their new challenges.

DAVID'S STORY

David told himself that he would be very unhappy having to visit his mom only on the weekends. He thought his social life would be disrupted and might not be on the soccer team that year. David started having a hard time getting out of bed in the morning and paying attention in class. He didn't even hang out with his friends or feel like playing video games with them. His grades started dropping, and eventually his friends stopped calling.

with a Gift ~
PEACE of Mind
So & Heart
don't be
Troubled
or Afraid John 14:27

SOPHIA'S STORY

Sophia was also very upset about her parents' divorce. She felt very angry and sad, however, Sophia told herself different things than David did. Sophia told herself that even though this was a big change in her life, she still had a lot of things to be happy about. She chose to learn from her parents' mistakes and made different choices about love and dating relationships. She was grateful to not hear them argue all the time, now that they were living in separate places. Sophia talked to certain friends when she was sad, but she did not let her family drama get in the way of having fun at times. She was able to put her feelings aside and continued to go out with friends. Sophia liked writing her feelings in a journal when it became hard to concentrate on schoolwork. This helped her process her thoughts and put it aside so that she could focus on other things.

Fix your thoughts On what is true & honorable RIGHT & PURE Lovely & Admirable. Think about things that are Excellent & Worthy of Praise
Phil. 4:8

Your attitude is a powerful tool, which only you can control. List 3 negative thoughts you have about the divorce and list 3 positive thoughts that could replace them.

NEGATIVE THOUGHTS	replaced with	Positive Thoughts

The Bible tells us to hold every thought captive in 2 Corinthians 10:5.

What do you think that means?

_____

_____

_____

What does Philippians 4:8 say about what we should think about?

_____

_____

_____

What scriptures could help you replace negative thoughts with positive thoughts?

_____

_____

_____

CHAPTER 11

Will It Ever Feel Normal Again?

"My stepfather came into my life at age seven. When I participated in activities he enjoyed (namely sports), we had something of a relationship. As I got older, he grew to resent me. He claims that my mom told him we have a father and he felt he had no rights to discipline us. My mom kept herself in the middle of his relationship with me and my brother. From ages 10–18 (and even now when I visit) he does not speak to me. He pretends I am not there and speaks of me in third person. When I do speak, he sighs and rolls his eyes. It's so difficult not to have any control over the climate you live in.

"I didn't realize until years later that I resented my mom for not helping make the relationship with my stepfather better. While it was not ideal (my stepdad ignoring me and my mom turning a blind eye), the situation helped lead me to place my faith in God. My physical needs were never a concern, but I had to trust in God for my emotional needs. I had a strong youth group and healthy adults and peers in my life. I observed caring marriages and warm family environments that kept me hopeful that it was possible for me as I started my own family. While my family did not provide everything I needed, God was faithful in providing what I needed through others."

GOD DECIDED IN ADVANCE *to adopt us* INTO HIS OWN *family* BY BRINGING US TO *Himself* THROUGH *Jesus Christ*
EPH. 1:5

133

WILL IT EVER FEEL NORMAL AGAIN?

There is a new normal in your life and much of it is probably unwelcomed. Your family is not in your control and you have to find your way through the cloudy, confusion. Living without one of your parents on a daily basis is a big deal and it takes a lot of getting used to. Emotions run high and problems can escalate. Chances are it will never feel exactly like your original family did, but it can still be really good.

What do you do when you feel like you have less control, and you want things back the way they used to be?

FIGURING IT OUT

Try to remember that you are not the only one trying to figure out how this new family is going to get along. Give everybody a little extra grace while you all get used to living together.

I really do believe God wants to help make your unique family work. He will provide strength and direction for your transition. It's important to remember that things don't work automatically. It will take time to build relationships and connect with one another. Be patient, hang in there, and trust that it will get better with time.

SINGLE PARENTS

• •

What thoughts do you have about your current family situation?

_____

_____

_____

_____

What do you worry about the most?

Examples: less time with parent(s), less money for extras, divided loyalty, wanting parents to reunite, having to be responsible for younger siblings?

_____

_____

_____

_____

What are some possible solutions to your situation or how can you handle your fears?

(Communicate your fears in a non-threatening way, get a part-time job to help with your extras, talk about your right to love and respect both parents, come up with a "game plan" to help out with the extra chores/responsibility.)

_____

_____

_____

_____

MY PARENT IS DATING AGAIN! GROSS!

It may be super awkward to think of your parent dating, but it's a reality that may happen at some point. Since your mom and dad are probably going to start dating again, it's good to prepare yourself for the possibility that they will get married again someday, too. This is a big change that may or may not happen for a while, or it may be happening for you right now.

Are one or both of your parents dating?

_____

_____

_____

How do you feel about it?

_____

_____

_____

Learning to love again after being hurt is risky and brings up a lot of fear and apprehension for you and your dating parent(s). God wants us to give and receive love. Your parents deserve to find love again, too.

Things to remember: Just because your parent(s) are dating again doesn't mean you become less important. You may have been the center of attention while your parent was single, but you can't expect that you will always be their only focus.

Discuss with your parent(s) if, when, and how you will meet the new person in their life.

Once you have had a chance to see the new relationship in action, make sure you wait and pray to God before making a hasty judgement. God can help you get His perspective on the situation and give you peace as you adjust to this new normal.

If you do like the new person in your mom's or dad's life, you don't have to consider yourself disloyal to the other parent.

A NEW STEPPARENT

Stepfamilies vary greatly. Some can be filled with many blessings, if you work intentionally together. Stepfamilies need time to adjust (they say it takes 5–7 years) to new living conditions, different parenting styles, along with rules and responsibilities. Developing trust and boundaries with one another is essential.

> ***Bear with each other*** *and forgive one another*
> *if any of you has a grievance against someone.*
> *Forgive as the Lord forgave you.*
>
> —COLOSSIANS 3:13

What does it mean to bear with each other?

_____

_____

_____

WHAT DO I CALL THEM?

As your stepfamily begins the process of bonding and forming its own identity, the names or terms you use to refer to one another are important.

What do you prefer to call your stepparent? When do you plan to talk to your parent about your decision?

_____

_____

_____

Did you come up with an agreed upon solution together and discuss it with your stepparent?

(Maybe start by using his or her first name. Eventually you may feel close enough to use "Mom" or "Dad," but you don't have to. If you feel pressured to call a stepparent "Mom" or "Dad," talk about it and respectfully share why you are not comfortable with it.)

_____

_____

_____

In public, how will you introduce your stepparent?

_____

_____

_____

How do you want them to introduce you?

_____

_____

_____

DO I HAVE TO LIKE THEM?

What do you like about your stepparent?

_____

_____

_____

Is there anything about them you wish were different?

_____

_____

_____

Technically you don't have to like anyone. There are going to be things about your new stepparent that you don't like, things that bug you, and things that are different than you are used to. But give them a chance. Different is not always a bad thing. Out of respect for your parent, be respectful and give yourself time to get to know them in a variety of situations before making a final decision. Try not to appear cold and aloof when meeting your parent's new partner. Ask God to help you be considerate and friendly. Keep an open mind and don't be too quick to pass judgement.

Love must be sincere.
Live in **HARMONY** with one another
As far as it depends on you,
Live at **PEACE** with everyone.
Rom. 12:9,18

What do the verses in Romans encourage you to do?

_____

_____

_____

You may not like this advice but pray *for* your stepparent daily—don't just pray *about* him/her. You must pray *for* him/her. They are not your enemy. When your prayers reflect a growing appreciation for them, God will soften your heart.

IS MY STEPPARENT ALLOWED TO BOSS ME AROUND?

Depending on your age, your stepparent plays a part in raising you and will be correcting you as needed. At first you may view the stepparent like a coach, mentor, or friend. They are part of your life, but not in a significant role yet. At first, they simply offer support and encourage positive values in your life. Eventually, with more time spent as a family, they become more like an aunt or uncle. They have more authority as a family member, but not quite the same as a parent.

Maybe they want you to keep up your room a certain way, fold the towels a certain way, or clean the kitchen every day. These changes are going to be hard to adjust to in a new home, but not impossible. Hopefully your parents will talk this through and come up with a plan that is best for everyone involved.

Discipline is part of loving someone when you have their best interest at heart. God wants the best for you, and though He admonishes parents to not provoke their children to anger, He also says He disciplines those He loves. God wants to show your parents how to parent you the best way possible.

Fathers DO NOT **provoke** your children to *ANGER* BY THE WAY YOU TREAT THEM. *Rather* BRING THEM UP with the **discipline** & *instruction* & that comes from the **Lord.**
Eph. 6:4

How would you want your parents to discipline you?

_____

_____

_____

_____

_____

DOES IT FEEL LIKE A BALANCING ACT?

· ·

Do you currently live in one or two homes? _____

Do you have a calendar to record your schedule? _____

Do you have a good working system in place to keep track of dates, events, holidays, commitments, schoolwork, sports, etc.?

(Depending on how old you are now, you may or may not have much say about how your time is split between your parents. If you are older, you may begin to make some of those decisions for yourself.)

_____

How do you balance your time between two families?

_____

_____

_____

Where do you spend your summers?

_____

_____

_____

Where will you be on Christmas or Easter? Birthdays—will you have one party or two?

_____

_____

_____

BACKPACK

• •

Prepare a backpack that has all the stuff you need and want, to make sure it gets taken from one house to the next.

What are your must-haves for your everything backpack?

☐ medications	☐ toothpaste	☐ vitamins
☐ cash	☐ dental floss	☐ underwear
☐ sunglasses	☐ soap	☐ socks
☐ eye mask	☐ deodorant	☐ sleepwear
☐ ear plugs	☐ shampoo	☐ jeans
☐ phone charger	☐ sunscreen	☐ shorts
☐ iPad	☐ contact lenses	☐ shirts
☐ lip balm	☐ nail clippers	☐ swimsuits
☐ gum	☐ lotion	☐ sandals
☐ hair brush	☐ tweezers	☐ snacks
☐ toothbrush	☐ pain relievers	☐ pillow

WHAT IS A BLENDED FAMILY?

When two families intertwine, it's called a Blended Family. At first, living in a blended family is going to be a really big adjustment. Mixing two families into one is not an easy thing to do, and it brings lots of unique challenges. Where will you sleep this weekend? Whose rules do you have to follow? And why do you have to treat these new kids like they're your brothers and sisters when they're really not?

While everyone is getting used to each other, you can count on a few tense moments. Over time, your new blended family will become more comfortable. Chances are it will never feel exactly like your original family did, but it can still be really good.

Are you currently living in a blended family? _____

What are the positive things you like about it?

_____

_____

_____

What are the challenging things that can make your blended family difficult?

_____

_____

_____

66 Seeing one another as a gift—yes, sometimes a frustrating gift— moves your heart in the direction of gratitude."

—Ron L. Deal

Gratitude has a way of softening our hearts toward one another. You can find ways to show empathy and compassion when you understand the value of gratitude in your family.

FIGURING IT OUT

· ·

The list provided below describes different aspects of living in two houses that you may not like. Rate each item from 1–5 to tell how much it bothers you. (1=very little and 5=very much). And on the right column write how long you think it will take to get used to this situation.

Having to leave friends on certain days.	1 2 3 4 5	_____
Watching parents argue when they drop you off.	1 2 3 4 5	_____
Having to remember different rules at each house.	1 2 3 4 5	_____
Having to pack your things all the time.	1 2 3 4 5	_____
Feeling like you can never relax and stay in one place.	1 2 3 4 5	_____
Having to remember what to bring from house to house.	1 2 3 4 5	_____
Having to remember two addresses.	1 2 3 4 5	_____
Being comfortable in one house but not the other.	1 2 3 4 5	_____
Having your social life interrupted.	1 2 3 4 5	_____
Not having friends near you at one house.	1 2 3 4 5	_____
Being away from a loved pet.	1 2 3 4 5	_____
Not getting to eat what you want when you want.	1 2 3 4 5	_____
Having to share with siblings.	1 2 3 4 5	_____
Having guests or neighbors stop by that you don't like or don't know.	1 2 3 4 5	_____
Other: _____	1 2 3 4 5	_____

PRAYER REQUEST & PRAISE REPORTS

Write down prayer requests in the space provided and pray for one another during the week.

I know the Lord
is always with me.
I will not be
Shaken
for he is
Right beside me.

Psalm 16:8

CLOSING PRAYER

Dear God,

There are big changes happening in my family. I am worried about a lot of things and need your help. I feel like I have to carry the burden alone. Words like overwhelmed, confused, exhausted seem to describe where I am.

Those who **fear the Lord** are SECURE He will be a REFUGE for their *children*

Prov. 14:26

How do I let you carry my heavy load? Please show me how. I pray you give me patience when I need it and help me communicate my needs and feelings with my family. Thank you, God, that you are my Heavenly Father, and I can depend on you. Thank you that you adopted me, and I will never be alone, even when I feel lonely. In Jesus' name. Amen.

Do you think you have what it takes to prepare for your future relationships? The next lesson will equip you to face love, dating, and the opposite sex with practical tips and biblcal guidance.

GET THIS 2.0

You Are Chosen

Psalms 139:13–16 says, "You made all the delicate, inner parts of my body and knit me together in my mother's womb. Thank you for making me so wonderfully complex! Your workmanship is marvelous—how well I know it. You watched me as I was being formed in utter seclusion, as I was woven together in the dark of the womb. You saw me before I was born. Every day of my life was recorded in your book. Every moment was laid out before a single day had passed."

How does this truth from God's Word make you feel?

_____

_____

_____

BEFORE YOU EVEN KNEW YOUR NAME

God had a special calling over your life. He chose you to do great things in the world that no one else can do. The Omniscient God sees you as His masterpiece. He knows you from the inside out and you are extremely important to Him.

> **If you believe this is true for you, then can it be true for other people in your family too?**

WHERE DID YOU COME FROM ANYWAY?

Did you pick who your parents would be? Did you pick where you were born? Did you pick who your siblings would be? Did you pick where you live now? Was all of this chosen for you? By whom? Is it fair that you didn't have a say?

In our world today, there are 195 countries, approximately 6,500 languages and roughly 7.53 million people. It is estimated that every four seconds, a child is born. Although these numbers seem colossal, the day you were conceived, God knew you intimately and made great plans for your life. No one is alive by accident.

Scientists have calculated the odds and crunched the numbers on you. They took wars, natural disasters, and dinosaurs into account, and do you realize the odds of you being born into this generation, to your parents, with the DNA structure and exact body composition that you have, are 1 in 400 trillion? Isn't that amazing?

Every single person is important in the sight of God.

I knew you
Before I
formed you
in your mother's womb
Before you were
Born
I set you apart.
Jeremiah 1:5

CHAPTER 12

What About Love, Dating, and Relationships?

ANNA'S STORY

"We started dating in high school and have been together for seven years," Anna said about her relationship with Clayton. "We've both been intentional to stay connected to God first. We actively serve God by volunteering with middle school students every week, and we give each other space to spend quality time with God. We inspire each other to keep growing deeper.

"We also go to each other with questions, share prayer requests, and pray for each other. This is what a godly, dating relationship looks like. In the beginning, we made a commitment to remain physically pure. We set up our own boundaries to protect each other from temptation. One example is not to be alone at night together past a certain time. It isn't always easy, but our relationship is stronger because of the spiritual intimacy we share.

"Clayton proposed to me in December and we have been planning the wedding while I am in graduate school to become a psychologist. Even while I lived in another state, we both remained faithful to each other and to our spiritual growth. We can't wait to celebrate our love and commitment with family and friends June 2021. We have intentionally prepared for a firm foundation based on God's love and principles."

Love is PATIENT & KIND
1 Cor. 13:4

SHAKEN

Take a few minutes to notice what God has done to help you through your journey so far.

In what ways has the Bible provided insight for decisions and encouragement?

_____

_____

_____

How has God's Word and the support of others in this group helped you process your feelings about the divorce?

_____

_____

_____

What has God been showing you during your prayer time with Him?

_____

_____

_____

But the Lords's plans
stand firm forever
His Intentions
Psalm 33:11 can never be
Shaken

WHAT DOES A HEALTHY RELATIONSHIP LOOK LIKE?

Who are some couples from TV or movies that you admire?

_____

_____

_____

Do you know of any people who have a relationship you consider positive and healthy?

_____

_____

_____

What does a healthy relationship look like? (Make a list of qualities and characteristics.)

_____

_____

_____

In your opinion, what are the characteristics of an unhealthy relationship? (Make a list of qualities and characteristics.)

_____

_____

_____

WHAT IS LOVE?

Have you ever asked questions like, "How do I know what love is? How can I tell if he or she is the one? Is love a feeling that can last forever?" You are not alone in wondering. Here are some ways to tell the difference between true love and counterfeit love.

TRUE LOVE	COUNTERFEIT LOVE
It is unconditional; it doesn't need to be earned	It requires you change to be accepted
It does not change, even when there is distance that separates	It is pushy, demanding, and unwilling to wait
It is willing to wait	It is more concerned with self; selfish
It does not insist on "my way" without concern for the wants of others	It is willing to tell lies to make itself look better
It is honest, and not misleading	It holds grudges and bitterness; It is rude and does things to make the other person feel bad about themselves
It forgives quickly	It is not faithful when distance separates
It is kind and respectful	It is jealous when others succeed
It desires the best for the other person	It resists giving and withholds blessings
It gives generously	It is noncommittal and will deny that there is a relationship with others
It is committed and does not hide the relationship	It works hard to try to get one's way
It does not control or manipulate to try to get one's way	It will manipulate and cheat to win
It protects and does not hurt others on purpose	It protects self-first
It brings peace and a sense of confidence in people	It brings embarrassment, hurt, and kills self-confidence in other people

FILL YOUR LOVE TANK

True love comes from God. When two people who love God first and each other second, their relationship is built on a firm foundation. When our hearts are connected to God, we are able to love others the way God intended us to. When we become lovers of God first, our hearts (love tanks) fill up, then they will overflow to others. The Bible says we should not be unequally yoked to someone who is not a believer of Jesus—this means we are to find another person who is equally as in love with God as we are.

What do you think about being equally yoked with your future boyfriend/girlfriend?

_____

_____

_____

Why would this be important to God?

_____

_____

_____

If his/her love tank is full and he/she is complete as a single person, he/she will be able to love you completely because God's love is in her/him. The healthiest relationships happen when two people want to grow spiritually in wisdom and knowledge of God and want to spur each other towards love and good deeds.

How is God's love filling your love tank these days?

_____

_____

_____

What are some ways we can keep our love tank full for God?

_____

_____

_____

5 PHASES OF A RELATIONSHIP

···

1. Attraction

Boys and girls are visually attracted to one another. They may start texting, talking, and hanging out with others.

2. Uncertainty

Each individual starts weighing the pros and cons of the relationship.

3. Exclusivity

It's Facebook official. Both people publicly commit to a monogamous relationship.

4. Intimacy

The couple becomes more physically affectionate and emotionally shares on a deeper level. Spiritual couples pray with and for each other, too.

5. Engagement

He actually proposes marriage and a lifetime commitment before God and family. She says yes! He puts a ring on her finger. They plan a date and start premarital preparation classes.

GUYS AND GIRLS APPROACH DATING VERY DIFFERENTLY

GIRLS FIRST:

Based on your past experience or from what you've observed from friends, in what order do you apply the 5 Phases of a Relationship?

_____

_____

_____

How do you think guys approach the 5 Phases?

_____

_____

_____

Most girls typically enjoy attention from a boy, ANY BOY! They feel special and wanted the minute a boy pays attention to them. Girls are immediately attracted to boys who give them positive attention. This starts Phase 1.

Girls skip Phase 2, the uncertainty phase, and disregard warnings and red flags from friends and family.

After a kiss, hand holding, and maybe a date, the girl assumes they are dating, and she calls him her boyfriend.

She feels vulnerable but trusts he will be with her for a long time. She thinks they are in Phase 3 and committed to being together. The intimacy and expectations grow quickly without him stating his intentions. She is already in Phase 4 as she shares more of her heart with him. Now she is on an emotional high and daydreaming about a future together. Thinking about colors for the wedding, doodling her name with his last name, starting a new wedding board on Pinterest, etc., are signs her heart is invested.

> Can you relate? How do you see relationships developing?

UNDERSTANDING OUR DIFFERENCES IN RELATIONSHIPS

Have you ever had your heart broken?

It feels like no amount of ice cream will make the pain go away. Some of us even feel physical pain in our chest when promises are broken, and dreams are crushed.

Learning how guys approach the 5 Phases of a Relationship has revolutionized how girls see dating teenage boys. Here's how boys approach the dating scene.

Phase 1: they are attracted to a pretty, sweet girl who laughs at their jokes. They start following her on social media and eventually get the courage to text her. They typically send out several texts to girls, just to see who will respond and how many they can "hit on" at a time.

He may ask a girl out or just show up somewhere she happens to be. As he continues to flirt, he tests the boundaries by touching and playing around. Maybe they go out a few times and hold hands, before the kissing starts happening. He begins sharing more about himself and is focused on getting as intimate as the girl will allow. This may go on for several weeks or even months without talking about defining the relationship. He doesn't want to get hung up on boyfriend/girlfriend titles. If she starts demanding more and more of his time, Phase 2 often kicks in.

When he hits Phase 2, the Uncertainty Phase, he weighs the pros and cons of being with this girl. At this stage, he may realize she is really getting on his nerves or he's bored with the whole thing and wants to move on to another cute girl from another class.

HERE IS WHERE THE PROBLEM LIES

Guys are mentally only in Phase 1 or Phase 2 the whole time! Even though their actions are telling girls something different, they really stay in the attraction phase for quite a long time. Girls, on the other hand, tend to skip Phase 2 altogether and rush into fast forwarding the friendship into a relationship, way before the guy makes his intentions known.

What About Love, Dating, and Relationships?

USE THESE WORDS TO FILL IN THE BLANKS.	
faking	soon
slow down	enjoy
history	love
red	time
dreaming	wait
observe	know
liking	group

1. The advice I give to girls is to _____! "Hold every thought captive to the obedience of Christ," is what the Bible says.

2. Don't assume things and start _____ about a lifetime together.

3. Enjoy the attraction phase and get to know different guys in a _____ setting.

4. _____ things for a long time and wait for the guy to show his true character, not just what he wants you to see.

5. Pay attention to the _____ flags.

6. Listen to your friends when they warn you of his _____ with other girls.

7. Ask yourself if you really have that much in common or if you are _____ it to make him more interested in you.

8. Don't manipulate a guy into _____ you. What you win him with is what you will have to keep him with, too.

9. Hold fast to your standards and _____ patiently for these guys to grow up.

10. Enjoy this season to get to know who you are and give yourself _____ to meet a variety of different people.

11. The advice I give to guys is to not lead a girl on until you _____ your intentions.

12. The Bible says, "Do not awaken _____ before it so desires" (Song of Solomon 2:7).

13. Hold off on too much intimacy too _____.

14. _____ the attraction phase and get to know a variety of girls before you decide who you want to be serious with.

> **"How do you know if he or she is the one?"**
> **How would you answer this question?**

There is no perfect answer. Love is a risk we have to be willing to take, but if you apply some of the biblical principles that define what real love is, you will be able to recognize when someone is acting unloving.

❝ You are not bound to make the same mistakes as your parents. It's important to know that your parents are human and make mistakes, too. You shouldn't hate them based off their mistakes and pick sides in a divorce. Everyone is doing the best they can. It's important to identify what "love" means and what it should look like. It may not be the love the world tells us it should look like." *–Rachel, 22*

WHEN IS IT TIME TO START DATING?

It's a different choice for everyone, but here are some interesting facts discovered over the years.

- The younger you are when you start dating, the more likely you are to have sex before marriage.

- 50% of dating relationships end in the first 90 days.

- The younger you are when you start dating, the more likely you are to become pregnant or get someone pregnant before marriage.

- The younger you are when you start dating, the more likely you are to get divorced.

This doesn't mean these things will happen to you if you start dating, it just means it's more likely to happen. Even adults haven't figured out this whole dating thing, but if you decide to start dating in middle or high school, here are some tips to help you do it well.

4 TIPS TO HELP YOU KNOW WHEN TO DATE

TIP #1: THERE'S SAFETY IN NUMBERS.

A group date is when you go out with a group of friends with your special guy/gal. Group dating is safer than a solo date for lots of reasons. It helps keep things from getting too serious too quickly and you get to see how they interact with other people publicly. What are some other positive reasons to date in groups?

TIP #2: AVOID THE TERM BOYFRIEND AND GIRLFRIEND.

It adds a bunch of pressure and expectations to the friendship. You will avoid things like going too far physically, hurting someone's feelings, dealing with jealousy, and the heartache that comes with breakups if you wait. It's expensive for boys who tend to pay for everything and is time consuming and distracting from other interests and people you care about.

TIP #3: NEVER START DATING UNLESS YOUR PARENTS SAY IT'S OKAY.

Dating is serious business. You should be open and honest with your parents and never do anything behind their backs.

TIP #4: WAIT TO DATE.

If the purpose of dating is to find a spouse, are you really ready for the commitment and responsibility of starting a family and making a life together? What's wrong with waiting until you are older and wiser?

WHAT IF I LOVE MY BOYFRIEND/ GIRLFRIEND MORE THAN GOD?

God wants to be your first priority. Does that sound selfish? Is that too much to ask of us for all He gives? Does that make God _____? (you fill in the blank, what word would you pick?)

It's possible to love your boyfriend/girlfriend more than God, your future spouse more than God, your future kids more than God, money more than God, your car more than God, your career more than God, or your reputation more than God. You name it. A lot of things can get between us and God. It's called idolatry and it's a sin. It's about loving something too much. That's why the tenth commandment is there!

TEN COMMANDMENTS

1. You shall have no other gods before me.
2. No carved images or likenesses.
3. Do not take the Lord's name in vain.
4. Remember to keep holy the Lord's day.
5. Honor thy father and thy mother.
6. Thou shalt not kill.
7. Thou shalt not commit adultery.
8. Thou shall not steal.
9. Thou shall not covet thy neighbor's wife.
10. Thou shall not covet they neighbor's goods.

My purpose is to give them a **Rich & Satisfying** *life.*
John 10:10

The first four commandments refer to our relationship with God. The next six commandments refer to our relationship with others. Our Heavenly Father doesn't want us to worship other gods. He doesn't want us to use His name carelessly. And He doesn't want us to forget to honor Him. The other commandments are sins that have one thing in common; they are all rooted in idolatry.

When we love something more than God, we may lie, cheat, steal, or kill for it. These are all sins against God. We may "covet" which mean to desire or crave something or someone that does not belong to us.

How can you love God more than anything? God Himself will use whatever means He must to keep us from loving something else more than Him. He will take away our health to make us take time to rest and heal.

He will keep His children absolutely secure to keep us from idolatry, because He loves us and wants us to have a full and abundant life. He does not want to keep love from us, but to enable us to love deeply, selflessly, and with full abandon—with no fear.

Does your focus on your boyfriend/girlfriend increase or decrease your love for God?

_____

_____

_____

How does he/she encourage your faith in God?

_____

_____

_____

How does he/she help you know God better?

_____

_____

_____

Do you both support each other's commitment to God and share the same values?

_____

_____

_____

PRAYER REQUEST & PRAISE REPORTS

Write down prayer requests in the space provided and pray for one another during the week.

Stand firm
in this grace
& you will be
unshakable

Based on 1 Peter 5:9-12

CLOSING PRAYER

Dear God,

I need you to fill my love tank. I feel conflicted at times about love, dating, and relationships. Please take away my doubts and confusion. Help me make wise choices. I need your wisdom and discernment to be able to protect my mind and heart. I want to honor you with my relationships.

Make me truly happy
BY AGREEING **wholeheartedly**
with each other. *loving*
one another, **&** working
Together
with one mind **&purpose.**

Phil. 2:2

I need your help and patience to wait for the right timing and the right person. Help me to enjoy getting to know many people and be open to love others the way you want me to love. In Jesus' Name. Amen.

Take a deep breath. You made it this far and we just have one more chapter to go! This is the most important one because it will set you up for a healthy relationship in your future.

This is Your Season

~~~~~~

God put Adam to sleep while he created Eve. Adam did not have to search for her because when Eve was ready, *He brought her to the man* (Genesis 2:22).

Young men can choose to rest in God, wait for God's timing, and prepare to become who God created them to be. If you have peace with God and have sought godly counsel in making a decision to pursue a young lady, then go for it.

EVE TIME

• •

In Genesis, we see that God made Adam out of dust, put him to sleep, and took his rib to create Eve.

But for Adam no suitable helper was found. So the LORD God caused the man to fall into a deep sleep; and while he was sleeping, he took one of the man's ribs and then closed up the place with flesh. Then the Lord God made a woman from the rib he had taken out of the man, and he brought her to the man.

—GENESIS 2:20–22

How long do you think it took God to make Eve? The Bible doesn't say if it took a day, a week, a month, a year, or more—but just imagine that time Eve had alone with God. She was not concerned or even aware of Adam or the earth God created. She was totally focused on God and only God for that season of time. She was not thinking about how to get a boyfriend, who she would date, who she would marry, etc. All those unknowns can make a girl crazy and discontent.

What if you approach this season of being single as a gift called Eve Time? During Eve Time you can learn:

- Who God is
- How to love Him and others
- What your purpose in life is
- Who God created you to be

God wants you to enjoy your relationship with Him in every season of life. This is your time to focus on His plan for your future.

CHAPTER 13

God's Purpose for Marriage

DEBRA'S STORY

"My heart's desire was to be married and have a family one day. I prayed for someone who loved God more than I did and who would love me unconditionally. I had fears about marriage. I didn't know if someone could love me if they really knew all my flaws and past mistakes. I remember telling God He would have to bring the right man to me. I didn't know if he would find me at church, waitressing at Cracker Barrel, or working at the crisis pregnancy center. Wouldn't you know he came into the pregnancy center!

"Steve was a youth pastor for a local church looking for a woman to speak to the girls in his youth group about love, dating, and purity. That was part of what I did for the pregnancy center. Since our first meeting, we became friends, and three months later we started dating. Steve and I had so much in common. When he asked me, "How's your walk with God?" I knew he was the right guy for me. We both served in student ministry for over ten years before we even met. While we were dating, we continued serving together in our church working with teenagers. He proposed to me in October and we married the following April.

"Today, we continue to help teenagers and serve God together. It has been an amazing adventure over the past sixteen years. We are still in the attraction phase! Our life mission is to point people to God and help each other accomplish every good work God has prepared for us to do."

A man leaves HIS FATHER AND MOTHER and is joined to his wife & THE TWO ARE united into one.
GEN. 2:24

Leaders: Begin this week by reviewing the highlights from previous lessons. Is there any topic that was not covered that the students have questions about regarding love, dating and relationships? You may want to discuss next steps for the students and help them take actions toward continued growth and healing. The group can discuss the option of planning a celebration for completing this workbook together. You could provide certificates of completion, have them evaluate the course anonymously, and share a meal together.

WHAT IS THE PURPOSE OF MARRIAGE?

Why do you think people get married?

_____

_____

_____

What are the benefits of marriage?

_____

_____

_____

Do you want to get married one day? Why or why not?

_____

_____

_____

USE THESE WORDS TO FILL IN THE BLANKS.

together

lifetime

meet

oneness

before

PURPOSE #1: MIRROR GOD'S IMAGE

1. God joined a man and a woman so that _____they would mirror His image.

2. Their _____ reflects the character and unity of God.

3. Their oneness is expressed within a _____commitment to each other. Couples who mirror God's image experience oneness in their marriage.

God created MAN in His own image, IN THE IMAGE OF GOD **He created him;** **Male** female HE CREATED THEM.
Gen. 1:27

PURPOSE #2 MUTUALLY COMPLETE ONE ANOTHER

1. Companionship in marriage is God's provision to replace isolation and _____ our deep longing for a close, intimate relationship.

2. Oneness in marriage is only possible when we put the needs of our spouse _____ our own needs and wants.

Don't be SELFISH Don't try to impress others **Don't look out** for your own interests. BUT TAKE AN INTEREST **in others too.**
Phil. 2:3

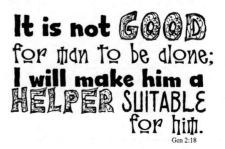
It is not GOOD for man to be alone; I will make him a HELPER SUITABLE for him.
Gen 2:18

PURPOSE #3: MULTIPLY A GODLY LEGACY

USE THESE WORDS TO FILL IN THE BLANKS.
Team
Multiply
Home
Children
Gift

1. Marriage is part of God's divine plan for two people to have

    _____.

    Then God blessed them & said, be fruitful AND MULTIPLY. Fill the earth & govern it. Reign over the fish in the sea, the birds in the sky, and ALL THE ANIMALS THAT SCURRY along the ground.
    Gen. 1:28

2. Oneness in marriage is necessary in order to _____ a godly legacy.

3. Neither women nor men are made emotionally, spiritually, or physically to raise children by themselves. Child rearing requires a _____ effort.

4. The roles of husband and wife are best understood by children as their parents model a peaceful marriage in their _____.

5. Couples who value children as a _____ from God can experience the blessing of a godly legacy.

Unbiblical Concepts Regarding Marriage	Biblical Concepts Regarding Marriage
Error:	Truth:
Marriage should be based upon romantic feelings of love. Marriage should be 50/50 partnership. You only do as much as your spouse does for you. When two people marry, they will or should remain the same over time. They will never change.	Marriage should be based upon biblical love which is not primarily a feeling but an action. Biblical love is choosing to do what is in the best interest of the other person, both give 100%. Marriage should result in both people growing and changing for the better.

WHAT FACTORS TRY TO BREAK MARRIAGES APART?

66 Satan knows that one of the greatest influences on your life is your family, and if he can mess it up, he will likely get you as well. But if you dedicate your family to God, you're well on your way to finding strength and answers you need to make your family successful. Satan would much rather see you distracted, discouraged and defeated!"

—RON L. DEAL, *THE SMART STEPFAMILY*

Satan's purposes are threatened by couples who are becoming one, therefore, Satan concentrates his major attacks on them.

For we are not fighting against FLESH-&-BLOOD ENEMIES, but AGAINST EVIL RULERS & authorities of the unseen world, against *mighty powers* IN THIS DARK WORLD, & against evil spirits in the **heavenly places.**

EPH 6.12

SHAKEN

USE THESE WORDS TO FILL IN THE BLANKS.
unity problems disappointment moving selfish deserve hinders

1. Every marriage is either _____ toward oneness or drifting toward isolation.

2. Difficult adjustments like contrasting backgrounds and different expectations _____ two people from remaining committed to one another.

3. Our culture's pattern to view relationships based on the 50/50 performance is unhealthy. It leads to unmet expectations, _____, and unbalanced unity in the relationship.

4. A failure to anticipate and respond to certain difficulties and _____ as they arise.

5. Withdrawing from each other causes feelings of rejection and more isolation instead of oneness and _____.

6. Our culture encourages the belief that we deserve complete fulfillment and _____ happiness from life and if someone is in the way of that happiness, it's their fault, and we should walk away.

7. Our selfish nature focuses on our spouse's weaknesses, mistakes, or failures to meet our unrealistic expectations. _____ behavior is destructive in relationships.

PREPARING FOR THE MARRIAGE

• •

Let's pretend you are planning your wedding celebration, what could be difficult about that? Unfortunately, the enemy is right there trying to steal, kill, and destroy the joy you were feeling the moment you got engaged.

Why is it a spiritual battle?

Satan has been trying to destroy marriages since Adam and Eve got together. He knows the power of two people unifying and representing the character of God to the world. God has the attributes of both male and female since both genders are made in His image.

Marriage is to reflect God's love to the world. Out of that love you create life, and that life is destined by God Himself. There is destiny and purpose to your marriage and your future children!

Your wedding is one day. I can hear Monica Gellar from *Friends* yelling at Chandler Bing about their wedding, "If you call our wedding a party one more time!"

I know a wedding is more than just a party. If you're a girl, it's probably something you have been dreaming of since you watched your first princess movie. Here is another perspective that may save you from becoming a Bridezilla leading up to the big day.

Stay focused on building a healthy foundation for your long-term relationship.

- What steps can you and your fiancé do to prepare for your marriage?
- Is there a mentor couple you can meet with once a week for dinner to talk through questions you may have?
- Is there a premarital group you could join?
- Is there a book you could read together and discuss with another engaged couple?

Investing in your relationship to keep it healthy and strong during the engagement phase is worth your time and will lead to long term success.

BIBLICAL ROLE OF A HUSBAND

. . . .

#1: A BIBLICAL HUSBAND MUST BE A SERVANT & LEADER.

This is a command, not a suggestion.

- A command to treat your wife as a treasure (valuable and delicate).

A treasure is highly valued and worth protecting. When the Bible says *the head of woman is man,* it does not mean male dominance. Dominance means a man demands a woman's total obedience to his every wish and command. God never viewed women as second-class citizens. His Word clearly states that we are all equally His children and are of the same value and worth before Him, as Galatians 3:28 tells us.

But there is one thing I want you to know: The head of every man **is Christ** The head of woman is man **the Head of Christ is God.**
1 Cor. 11:3

#2: A BIBLICAL HUSBAND LOVES HIS WIFE UNCONDITIONALLY.

Unconditional acceptance of your wife is not based upon her performance, but on her worth as God's gift to you. If you want to love your wife unconditionally, always be sure her emotional tank is full. One of the best ways to do that is to affirm her constantly. Let her know verbally and demonstratively that you value her, respect her, and love her. She is a treasure worthy of protecting and cherishing.

There is no longer Jew or Gentile slave or free, male & female For you are all one in *Christ Jesus.*
Gal. 3:28

#3: A BIBLICAL HUSBAND SERVES HIS WIFE.

Being head of your wife does not mean being her master, but her servant. Again, Christ is our

Submit to one another OUT OF REVERENCE FOR *Christ* For wives, this means submit TO YOUR HUSBANDS AS TO THE *Lord* For a husband is the head of his wife as Christ is the HEAD OF THE CHURCH.
EPH. 5:21-22

model for this type of leadership. Jesus did not just talk about serving; He demonstrated it when he washed His disciples' feet found in John 13.

IN THE SAME WAY, you husbands must give honor *to your wives* TREAT YOUR WIFE WITH understanding as you live together.

SHE MAY BE WEAKER THAN YOU ARE, but she is your equal partner in God's *gift of new life.*

TREAT HER AS YOU SHOULD so your prayers *will not be hindered.*
1 PET. 3:7

What do you think 1 Peter 3:7 is saying to husbands?

_____

_____

_____

What is the reward if you follow Peter's advice?

_____

_____

_____

66 The more inward you focus, the more miserable you will become. If you can only dwell on your unmet expectations, let downs, constant disappointments, and frustrations, you will be miserable. Focusing on yourself is nowhere in the Bible."

—Mrs. Francis Chan

SCUBA TANK

When you are a scuba diver, your air is limited under water. A married couple can't share one tank of air and survive. The tank represents your intimate relationship with God. You both need your own tank to be satisfied. The key is to find contentment in your relationship with God. He is the only one who can completely satisfy you. You will find life and satisfaction in Christ alone. You are not looking for someone else to give you a fulfilling life or complete you. When two people come together with a solid relationship with God, their tank is already full, and they won't drain each other. With two full tanks they help each other continue to stay close to God and grow in faith and intimacy together.

How full is your scuba tank these days?

_____

_____

_____

If you are feeling disconnected with God, what steps can you take to fill your tank?

_____

_____

_____

Name some couples that you have observed who have a full love tank and a healthy marriage.

_____

_____

_____

BIBLICAL ROLE OF A WIFE

#1: A BIBLICAL WIFE IS A HELPER TO HER HUSBAND.

Genesis tells us that God realized it wasn't good for man to be alone, and that He decided to make a *helper suitable for him* (Gen. 2:18 NIV). God has designed wives to help their husbands become all that God intends them to be.

#2: A BIBLICAL WIFE RESPECTS HER HUSBAND.

The wife must respect her husband (Ephesians 5:33). When you respect your husband, you notice him, regard him, honor him, prefer him, and esteem him. It means valuing his opinion, admiring his wisdom and character, appreciating his commitment to you, and considering his needs and values. Every husband wants his wife to be on his team, to coach him when necessary, but most of all to be his cheerleader. A husband needs a wife who is behind him, believing in him, appreciating him, and cheering him on as he goes out into the world every day.

#3: A BIBLICAL WIFE SUBMITS TO HER HUSBAND.

The controversial concept of submission has been highly debated and misunderstood. Some fear that submission leads to being used or abused. Another misconception is that submission means blind obedience on the part of the woman.

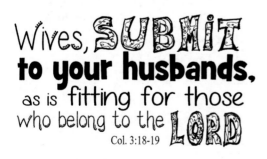

Wives, SUBMIT to your husbands, as is fitting for those who belong to the LORD
Col. 3:18-19

Submit to one another OUT OF REVERENCE FOR Christ For wives, this means submit TO YOUR HUSBANDS AS TO THE Lord. For a husband is the head of his wife as Christ is the HEAD OF THE CHURCH.
EPH. 5:21-22

Why do you think women are so offended by the term "submission?"

_____

_____

_____

What do you think God had in mind when He calls women to submit to their husbands?

_____

_____

_____

WHAT SUBMISSION IS NOT:

· ·

A wife must submit . . .

- Because she is inferior to man.
- Because her husband is perfect.
- Because she should not speak or question her husband.
- Because she should not try to influence her husband's decisions.

66 A wife should submit voluntarily to her husband's sensitive and loving leadership. She is helping him fulfill his responsibilities, and she helps him become the man, the husband, and the leader God intended him to be."

—Barbara Rainey

Submission is two words put together, "sub" and "mission." A woman is to come alongside her husband's mission. Whatever he is called by God to do, she is called to support and encourage. She takes on the supporting role to his mission in life. The husband does the same for his wife. It's an equal partnership.

DEALING WITH CONFLICT

Devon's parents divorced when he was younger. Now that he's been married two years, when asked what would you wish someone told you when you were a teenager to help prepare you for marriage? He said, "I wish I knew that fighting didn't mean they don't love you. I thought that if you fight, then the love is gone, and you should break up. I wish I knew how to handle conflict."

Conflict is common in all marriages. The goal of marriage is not to be conflict free but to handle conflict correctly when it occurs. Healthy conflict resolution occurs when couples are willing to seek and offer forgiveness. Refer to chapter 10 to review tips on handling conflict.

Conflict occurs when we don't get what we want, and this can lead to anger. Our unfulfilled desires lead to fighting and yelling. Being able to calm down and communicate clearly takes maturity and a commitment to oneness in the marriage. Approaching a conflict carefully requires the right timing and the right focus and should be done in love and humility. Your goal is to restore oneness in your marriage. Not to prove you are right or demand your way.

Make every effort TO KEEP YOURSELVES UNITED in the Spirit, BINDING YOURSELVES together with PEACE.

Eph. 4:3

SEEKING FORGIVENESS

1. Be willing to say you were wrong: "I was wrong, I shouldn't have . . ."

2. Be willing to say you are sorry: "I am sorry I did _____ , and that I caused you to feel _____."

3. Be willing to repent: "I know that I have hurt you deeply, and I do not wish to hurt you this way again."

4. Be willing to ask for forgiveness: "Will you forgive me for doing _____?"

GRANTING FORGIVENESS

You might think the most important three words are, "I love you." But when feelings are hurt and a couple needs to resolve tension and conflict, the best thing you can say is, "I forgive you." Granting forgiveness heals the soul for both people. We need to say it out loud to affirm one another and move forward.

1. Do it in prayer to God first: "God, I forgive _____ for hurting me."

2. Do it specifically: "I forgive you for _____."

3. Do it generously: "Let's settle this issue and get on with building our relationship."

4. Do it graciously: "I know I've done things wrong myself."

Refer to Chapter 9 for more tips on forgiving people.

We've covered a lot of new concepts regarding the purpose of marriage, the biblical roles of a wife and husband, submission, conflict, and forgiveness in a relationship. Discuss how this chapter impacted your view of marriage.

Are you more open to the idea of getting married one day?

_____

_____

_____

_____

_____

What would you do differently to protect your future marriage from divorce?

_____

_____

_____

_____

_____

Your parents splitting up or divorcing is a complicated and multifaceted event in your life and has impacted your whole family. Each member may continue to experience intense feelings of loss, sadness, grief, anger, loneliness, fear, and confusion, just to name a few. There also may be feelings of relief, hope, and freedom. You can help others in your family work through their emotions now that you have learned through the support of this group and the information in this workbook, how to cope better.

What is the biggest takeaway you want to remember from the past 13 lessons?

_____

_____

_____

_____

_____

How has God used this group and workbook to deepen your spiritual walk with Him?

_____

_____

_____

_____

_____

PRAYER REQUEST & PRAISE REPORTS

Write down prayer requests in the space provided and pray for one another during the week.

I know the Lord is always with me. I will not be **Shaken** for he is Right beside me.

Psalm 16:8

CLOSING PRAYER

Dear God,

Help me to stop worrying about my future. I want to trust that it is all in your hands. You are good and your plans for me are good. I need patience as I wait on your timing for things to work out. I want to stay in the center of your will and pray

You will keep in perfect **PEACE** HIM WHOSE mind is steadfast because he **TRUSTS** IN YOU.

Isaiah 26:3

you will guide my steps. Give me a vision for the future you have planned for me. Whether single or married one day, help me enjoy contentment in whatever season you have me in. You are my source of hope, peace, and love. Fill my love tank and make me whole. Please help me remember to spend time with you every morning. Awaken me each day with a desire to read your Word and stay connected to other believers. In Jesus' name, Amen.

Setting Goals

SETTING GOALS FOR YOUR FUTURE

We hope these past few weeks have given you the guidance, support, and hope you need, not to just survive your parents' divorce, but to really thrive in the midst of these circumstances. Just because your life might be difficult now doesn't mean it always will be. You could write in a journal about how you want your life to be in the future.

For example:

- What career do you want to pursue?
- Where do you want to live?
- Will you marry and have children some day?

SET NEW GOALS FOR YOURSELF

Make them realistic, specific and measurable, preferably with a deadline.

For example:

I'm going to get a job babysitting and work at it for at least two months, so I can have money to go to the movies and eat out with friends.

I am going to get neighbors to pay me to mow their lawns so I can make extra money for the holidays and buy gifts for Christmas.

I'm going to go to college to get a degree in family counseling, so I can help others who are struggling with family relationships. I want to use what I learned to help people.

SHAKEN

What are some goals you want to accomplish?

_____
_____
_____
_____
_____
_____
_____
_____
_____
_____
_____
_____
_____
_____
_____
_____
_____
_____
_____
_____
_____
_____
_____
_____
_____
_____
_____

Acknowledgements

To my family, teachers, mentors, students, and friends around the world whose lives have enriched my own in many ways. The pages of this workbook are inspired by the stories you have graciously shared with me. Thank you.

Thank you Chip and Carla Gill who led the first support group for teens dealing with divorce at Christ's Church. You understood the need and jumped in to help. Because of you this workbook was created.

Thank you, Steve and Kim Blake, who led your own group for teens at Christian Family Chapel. I am grateful for your heart for teens and the input you gave me to make this resource available for others.

Thank you, Brookstone Creative Group, for believing in the importance of this workbook, encouraging me along the way, and contributing your wisdom and talents to make this dream a reality.

Thank you, God, for inspiring me and compelling me to write this book. Thank you for the grace to persevere and provision of time, resources, and wisdom to create this work. May you be glorified through this and may many lives be impacted by your Holy Spirit.

Answer Key

Chapter 2

1. Focus
2. Sleep
3. Feel
4. Hear
5. Under
6. Alone
7. Moody
8. Numb
9. Fun
10. Sick

Chapter 3

1. Denial
2. Anger
3. Bargaining

Chapter 4

1. Depression
2. Blame
3. Acceptance
4. Forgiveness

Chapter 6

1. Cares
2. Sadness
3. View
4. Home
5. Sleep
6. Loss
7. Energy
8. Focus
9. Hopelessness
10. Feels

Chapter 7

1. Wrong
2. God
3. Feeling
4. Serious
5. Symptom
6. Peace
7. Quickly
8. Health

1. Safe
2. Hear
3. Relax
4. Calm
5. Slow

Chapter 8

1. Anger
2. Relax
3. Cause
4. Out
5. Listen
6. God
7. Bible
8. Learn

1. A Gentle Answer
2. Harsh Words
3. Others
4. More
5. Voice
6. Slowly
7. Listen
8. Fix
9. Age
10. Handle

Chapter 9

1. Debt
2. Control
3. Gift
4. Revenge
5. God's
6. Process
7. Good
8. Sin
9. Enabling
10. Apology
11. Covering
12. Forgetting
13. Trust
14. Lead

Chapter 10

1. Share
2. Happen
3. Problems
4. Safe
5. Plan

1. Always
2. Name
3. You
4. Out
5. Respond
6. Avoid
7. Threats
8. Positive
9. Focus
10. Topic
11. Body
12. Attention
13. Should
14. Good

Chapter 12

1. Slow Down
2. Dreaming
3. Group
4. Observe
5. Red
6. History
7. Faking
8. Liking
9. Wait
10. Time
11. Know
12. Love
13. Soon
14. Enjoy

Chapter 13

1. Children
2. Multiply
3. Team
4. Home
5. Gift

1. Moving
2. Hinders
3. Disappointment
4. Problems
5. Unity
6. Deserve
7. Selfish

Reference List

Anderson, Neil T. *The Steps to Freedom in Christ.* Grand Rapids, MI: Bethany House Publishers, 2017.

Biblical Counseling and Discipleship Training. Jacksonville, FL: The Hope Center, 2015.

Bonior Ph.D, Andrea. "Way To Build Trust In A Relationship." *Psychology Today,* December 2018, www.psychologytoday.com/us/blog/ friendship-20/201812/7-ways-build-trust-in-relationship.

Cassella-Kapusinski, Lynn. *Now What Do I Do?: A Guide to Help Teenagers with their Parents' Separation or Divorce.* Chicago: ACTA Publications, 2006.

Deal, Ron L. *The Smart Stepfamily: 7 Steps to a Healthy Family.* Grand Rapids, MI: Bethany House Publishers, 2002, 2014.

Grissom, Steve. *Divorce Care: Hope, Help, and Healing During and After Your Divorce.* Nashville, TN: Thomas Nelson Publishers, 2006.

Johnson, Kurt, and Mark Oestreicher. *My Family.* Grand Rapids, MI: Zondervan Publishers, 2007.

Oates, Elizabeth. *Dealing with Divorce: Finding Direction When Your Parents Split Up.* Grand Rapids, MI: Zondervan, 2001.

Rainey, Dennis and Barbara. "Staying Close." *FamilyLife,* 2002, www.familylife.com/articles/topics/marriage/staying-married/husbands/ what-should-be-the-husbands-role-in-marriage.

Schab, Lisa M. *The Divorce Workbook for Teens.* Oakland, CA: New Harbinger Publications, Inc., 2008.

Thesman, R.J. "10 Signs You Are Emotionally Overwhelmed and What to Do About It." *Crosswalk,* July 24, 2018.

Tracie Miles blog. May 9, 2012, "How to Handle Anger in a Biblical Way."

About the Author
Debra Burns

Debra Burns understands the confusion, fears, and pain a teenager feels when their parents divorce. She has spent twenty-five years leading teenagers to hope and healing through a relationship with Jesus Christ. After graduating from the University of Central Florida, Debra served with CRU High School Ministry, mentoring students, developing curriculum, and traveling around the world speaking at conferences. She is the President of Bloom (Biblically Living Out Our Mission) with Deb, which equips young women to discover and fulfill their purpose in life. Originally from Rochester, NY, she lives in Jacksonville, Florida, with her husband, Steve. Together they founded Examining Solutions and serve together at Christ's Church River City Campus. Debra has worked in a variety of roles within Christ's Church as Student Spiritual Formations Director and is currently the Community Care Pastor, leading support groups for teenagers and adults.

Subscribe to **Shaken by Debra Burns YouTube Channel** to enhance your experience while using this workbook. You will have access to extra bonus material from the author and learn about other recommended resources. Join with others on our Facebook community at "Shaken by Debra Burns."

Connect with the Author

www.debraburns.net